Untwisting Scriptures

THAT WERE USED TO TIE YOU UP, GAG YOU,
AND TANGLE YOUR MIND

Rebecca Davis

Justice Keepers Publishing
Tillamook, Oregon

Copyright © 2016 by Rebecca Davis

All rights reserved. No part of this publication may be reproduced, distributed or transmitted in any form or by any means, including photocopying, recording, or other electronic or mechanical methods, without the prior written permission of the publisher, except in the case of brief quotations embodied in critical reviews and certain other noncommercial uses permitted by copyright law.

For permission requests and quantity discounts, write to the publisher, Justice Keepers Publishing, through the website www.cryingoutforjustice.com.

All Scripture quotations, unless otherwise noted, are from the Holy Bible, English Standard Version® (ESV®), copyright © 2001 by Crossway, a publishing ministry of Good News Publishers. Used by permission. All rights reserved.

Cover photo by Stephanie Council
Cover design by Tim Davis
Book Layout ©2013 BookDesignTemplates.com

Untwisting Scriptures that were used to tie you up, gag you, and tangle your mind / Rebecca Davis. —first edition.
01 02 03 04 05 06 07 08 09

ISBN 978-0-9981981-0-1

*Dedicated to the people who have taught me,
including close friends, writers, and speakers.
But especially the close friends.
I hope you know how much I appreciate you.*

Contents

Foreword by Jeff Crippen 7

Introduction 9

Chapter 1 – I should "yield my rights" or maybe I never had any rights. 11
    How "yielding of rights" is often taught
        Anger is sinful and is caused by insisting on personal rights / The solution to anger (which is always sinful) is to yield all our rights, which means living as if we have no rights, like Jesus / When we yield our rights, then God will bless us and bring us joy
    "Human rights" is a vital concept
        What are "rights"? / Our nation was founded on "human rights" / Human rights in the Bible / Jesus always retained His rights / Paul's claim on his rights as a citizen
    Other Scriptures that address the idea of rights
        Scriptures showing human or civil rights can be violated / Scriptures showing we can refrain from "making use of" our rights

Chapter 2 – So I'm not supposed to "yield my rights"? 27
    What are the "no-rights" teachers missing?
        They fail to acknowledge genuine human and civil rights / They confuse vertical and horizontal relationships / They fail to distinguish rights from desires / They twist Scriptures to teach their "no-rights" doctrine
    Double standards are created
        The "no-rights" doctrine applies only to certain rights, not others / The "no-rights" doctrine applies only to certain people, not others
    Instead of thinking about "yielding rights" . . .
        We want our desires to be aligned with God's will / We want to live the Christian life by faith, not works
    Christians have specific rights in Christ
    Looking at our rights in a new light

Chapter 3 – I still feel the effects of the pain, so "I must be bitter" 47
    How Biblical "bitterness" is often preached
        They tell stories / They cite professionals / They define bitterness as unforgiveness and resentment / They say bitterness is hidden deep within an individual's heart / They say bitterness is caused by . . . / They say bitterness is the "root cause" of many other sins / What do they say is the solution?
    What does the word *bitterness* mean?

Sources of Bitterness in the Bible
Grieving Bitterness in the Bible
The feeling of agony and grief / The expression of agony and grief
Understanding grief
Grief has been ignored / What is grief? / Case study: Naomi / Case study: Job / Grieving bitterness is not sin / Grieving bitterness after abuse / Our Good Shepherd is with us in our grieving

Chapter 4 – I'm told I have a "root of bitterness" or I'm in the "gall of bitterness" 73

The "root of bitterness" in Hebrews
The Old Testament reference / Who was he speaking to? / What about the context?
The "gall of bitterness" in Acts

Chapter 5 – I'm afraid I'll be guilty of "Destructive Bitterness" 85

More Scriptures about Destructive Bitterness
Psalm 64:2-4 / Habakkuk 1:6 / Romans 3:14 / James 3:13-18 / Colossians 3:19 / Ephesians 4:29-32
Looking at Destructive Bitterness in a new light
A response to those who preach their own idea of bitterness
Is bitterness resentment, unforgiveness, and hostility? / Is bitterness hidden deep within an individual's heart? / Is bitterness caused by . . . / Is bitterness the "root cause" of almost every other sin? / What about the solutions given by the Scripture Twisters?
Responding rightly to bitterness

Chapter 6 – I shouldn't "take up offenses" for others 97

Bill Gothard's teaching on "taking up offenses"
That mysterious Psalm 15:3 reference / The Basic Seminar teaching / The background of that teaching
"Taking up offenses" in modern-day teachings
"Taking up causes" in the Bible
Direct admonitions in Scripture / Examples in Scripture
"Taking up causes" in history
"Taking up causes" in Christian families, churches, and ministries
Crying out for justice / Advocating in the Southern Baptist Convention / Advocating one soul at a time / If Christians fail to advocate?
Final thoughts

Final words 117

About the author 119

Foreword

Jeff Crippen

The Apostle Paul knew what it was to be bound by the teachings of Scripture twisters. Much of his writing in the New Testament is devoted to exposing and warning us of these very tactics. Yet most Christians do not seem to have taken these many warnings as seriously as they were given. Jesus Himself likewise issued the same kind of warnings: "Watch and beware of the leaven of the Pharisees and Sadducees" (Matthew 16:6).

In our ministry to abuse victims, we see the effects of this poisonous leaven every single day. And Rebecca Davis has seen it as well, far too many times. Genuine Christian men, women, young people, and even children are being tied up by widespread perversions of God's Word so that they are experiencing bondage instead of the freedom Christ has given His people.

> *For freedom Christ has set us free; stand firm therefore,*
> *and do not submit again to a yoke of slavery.*
> Galatians 5:1

Untwisting Scriptures is written to help Christ's sheep more clearly hear their Shepherd's voice. If you really know Christ, you will certainly recognize His truth in contrast to the lies you very probably have been taught, and sense the freedom He gives as you read what Rebecca has written.

Far too many of us have allowed a yoke of slavery to be put upon us as we listened to preachers, read popular Christian authors, and repeated their phrases to one another without carefully and prayerfully searching the Scriptures to see if these things be so. It is time we started digging in, asking questions, and letting the Spirit of Christ in us open our eyes and minds to see His Word in truth.

Are you confident that you know what the Bible says about "a root of bitterness"? Or about "taking up offenses"? Or "giving up your rights to follow Christ"? Hold your answer until you read this timely new book that has been given to the body of Christ.

Then go out and walk in the freedom Jesus intends you to have.

Jeff Crippen, pastor
Christ Reformation Church
Tillamook, Oregon
www.cryingoutforjustice.com

INTRODUCTION

A few words

Over the last ten years, in the course of meeting, getting to know, and walking with abuse survivors (both domestic abuse and sexual abuse), I began to hear more and more ways the Scriptures had been used to manipulate them and keep them in fear and bondage.

Spiritual abuse.

"But . . . that isn't what that means," I sputtered. "But . . . that's being taken out of context and . . . twisted."

Bit by bit I began to blog about some of the Scriptures in question. First a little. Then more. At some point someone suggested they should become a book. So here is one, addressing only a few of them. Maybe one day there will be another.

Many thanks to my pre-publication readers, several of whom were abuse survivors, who gave very valuable input. One of the things they suggested was that the wrong teachings be set off in some way to make it very clear that these are not the teachings that I espouse. So now they're in gray boxes, and if you find the wrong teachings bringing up some old unpleasant emotions, you can simply skip over them.

I appreciate the assistance of Hebrew scholar Sam Powell, who helped me rightly read some Old Testament passages. And of course to Jeff Crippen, who, with his colleagues at www.cryingoutforjustice.com, continues to Cry for Justice. And to Tim, for being there.

CHAPTER 1

I should "yield my rights" or maybe I never had any rights

Has anyone ever told you the Bible teaches that as a Christian you should surrender your rights? It might sometimes seem confusing, wondering if you even have any rights, or why it might seem like other people have rights when you don't.

When people are directly told that they need to give up their rights, it's often in a specific context. It could be like the case of a certain controlling pastor who told the people of his congregation where they needed to live—they needed to "give up their right" to choose where they lived. Or the case of another controlling pastor who told the people of his congregation how to organize their kitchen cabinets and which cars they should buy.

In both cases, "obedience to authority" trumped individual rights for these people to make their own decisions.

Or maybe instead of a controlling pastor, it was a controlling spouse. Maybe you were told in the name of submission or love, that you should "yield your rights" in the marriage. For example, if your husband wanted to call you foul names, you may have been told to "yield your rights" to be treated with dignity and respect.

There are also cases of children in Christian homes being told by their parents that they don't have any rights. One woman said that when she was growing up, as a child in her home she had no right to feel sad or angry, to expect safety, or to protect herself.

Somehow it might seem a little easier to see that other people should have rights, maybe a little harder to see it about yourself.

But when the Scriptures are untwisted, they'll present you with a whole new way of looking at this concept of *rights*.

How "yielding of rights" is often taught

The idea of "yielding your rights" has been taught in many different Christian contexts—so many that you may not have ever questioned it. Here are a few examples of the way it's presented. You may find that they feel familiar, but are they Scriptural? Are they *right*?

Don't lose hope as you read them—encouragement lies ahead!

– Anger is sinful and is caused by insisting on personal rights

> The root cause of extended anger is typically based on a "wrong" premise about "rights." . . . When we feel that our real or perceived "rights" have been violated, we can easily respond with anger.[1]

> All too often, I find myself annoyed and perturbed when things don't go my way. A decision someone makes at the office, a rude driver on the freeway, a long line at the checkout counter, a thoughtless word spoken by a family member, a minor offense (real or perceived) by a friend, someone who fails to come through on a commitment, a phone call that wakes me when I have just fallen off to sleep—if I am staking out my rights, even the smallest violation of those rights can leave me feeling and acting moody, uptight, and angry.[2]

> We all tend to demand our own way instead of prayerfully and humbly giving up certain rights. When we demand our rights or become focused on what we

---

[1] June Hunt, *Anger: Facing the Fire Within* (Rose Publishing, 2013), p 44.
[2] Nancy Leigh DeMoss, *Lies Women Believe and the Truth that Sets Them Free* (Moody Publishers, 2002), p 76.

> think we deserve, then we will live lives of frustration, anger, bitterness, and defeat.[3]

> Demanding your "rights" is pride in expecting that you deserve to be treated a certain way. Ultimately, we deserve nothing but judgment for our sin. When we pridefully demand our rights, there is always contention.[4]

> Just because you are alive, you probably believe you have the right to be accepted as an individual, to express opinions, to earn and spend a living, to control your personal belongings, and to make decisions. You expect others to respect your rights.[5]

Now, let's think about those statements for a minute.

Did you notice that the first two writers didn't think it even mattered whether your right was *real* or *perceived*? One writer said if you think you deserve to be treated a certain way, that's pride.

And all of them appear to think anger is always sinful.

Are those the kinds of teachings you're familiar with?

So then the "no-rights" teachers offer their solution. . . .

— The solution to anger (which is always sinful) is to yield all our rights, which means living as if we have no rights, like Jesus

> The heart of Jesus' teaching involves our willingness to surrender our rights in order to reveal Christ to the unsaved and to help mature our brothers and sisters. Paul repeatedly surrendered his rights in order to promote the gospel

---

[3] Karol Ladd, *A Woman's Passionate Pursuit of God: Creating a Positive and Purposeful Life* (Harvest House Publishers, 2011), p 84.

[4] Dan Leningen, "My 'Rights,'" Grace and Truth Bible Church, April 11, 2014, www.gtbchurch.org/posts/18778.

[5] "What is the principle of ownership?" Institute in Basic Life Principles. www.iblp.org/questions/what-principle-ownership. The implication here is that this is a wrong way of thinking.

> with others. We too must set aside our rights in order to promote the gospel and to magnify God to the world.[6]

> Kindness graces a wife with the ability to serve her husband without worrying about her rights.[7]

> But what are our legitimate rights? One person would answer, "Happiness." Another would say, "Freedom to live life my way." Yet this was not the mind-set of Jesus. He yielded His rights to His heavenly Father.[8]

> Meekness is taking our rights, *all of them*, and placing them on God's altar and saying, "God, from this day forward these are not my rights any more. These are Your rights. If You want to withhold them, I'll thank You for that. If You want to give them back to me, I'll thank You for that."[9]

Do you see that ultimately they're telling you that you're supposed to live as if you have no rights?

Then they say . . .

– *When we yield our rights, God will bless us and bring us joy*

> [I]f we are willing to give up our rights, we bless and bring peace to others and to ourselves.[10]

> When we surrender our rights and needs to God, we will receive back much more than we yield to Him.[11]

---

[6] Lorraine Hill, *Reclaiming Your Joy: A Bible Study on Conquering Your Joy-Stealers* (Tate Publishing, 2011), p 117.

[7] Stephen Kendrick and Alex Kendrick, *The Love Dare Day by Day: A Year of Devotions for Couples* (B&H Books, 2013), p 50.

[8] June Hunt, *Anger: Facing the Fire Within*, p 44.

[9] Bill Gothard, "Basic Seminar Session 8: How to Transform Irritations," www.embassymedia.com. Italics added.

[10] Ladd, *A Woman's Passionate Pursuit of God*, p 84.

> [Y]ielding our personal rights and expectations to Him helps us resolve irritations, anger, and worry.[12]

> Releasing your "rights" to be treated well, hold a grudge, or exercise your freedom of choice will bring you incredible peace and joy because you won't feel slighted when you are treated poorly. . . . Only when you release you rights will you have the mind of Christ, be able to walk in the Spirit, and see His fruit produced in your life.[13]

> I am convinced that the claiming of rights has produced much, if not most, of the unhappiness women experience today.[14]

> The truth is, when you relinquish your rights for the sake of your mate, you get a chance to lose yourself to the greater purpose of marriage.[15]

> [Eating] is not a right anymore, it's a privilege that you will receive and do for His glory. So we thank God for privileges, we don't demand them, but we give God our rights. If you give God your right to a good night's sleep, and then something awakens you tonight halfway through the night, you thank God for a half night's sleep. Or if He gives you a full night's sleep, you thank Him for the privilege of a full night's sleep.[16]

You may have an initial reaction of thinking there's something wrong with these statements, but not sure exactly what. You may feel concerned that your sinful, selfish heart is over-reacting to what you've always been taught to be true.

---

[11] Guillermo Maldonado, *Supernatural Transformation: Change Your Heart into God's Heart* (Whitaker, 2014), p 197.

[12] "What is the principle of ownership?" Institute in Basic Life Principles. www.iblp.org/questions/what-principle-ownership.

[13] Dan Leningen, "My 'Rights,'" www.gtbchurch.org/posts/18778.

[14] Nancy Leigh DeMoss, *Lies Women Believe*, p 74.

[15] Stephen Kendrick and Alex Kendrick, *The Love Dare Day by Day*, p 59. This could be seen as an example of exalting marriage dangerously close to idolatry.

[16] Bill Gothard, "Basic Seminar Session 8," www.ombanoymedia.com.

But it's absolutely appropriate to find these statements troubling—because this no-rights teaching leads straight into the hands of abusers.[17]

> *If you're being abused, how could you even be aware of it unless you can see that your rights are being violated?*

So the question is . . . *what's wrong with this teaching?* How can it be untwisted?

Well, we start by laying a foundation of "human rights."

For people who are "twisted up" by false teaching, it can often be easier to see what's true if you think about someone else in a situation similar to your own. Maybe if you're having trouble applying these truths to yourself, you could picture someone else as you read about human rights and think about *what is right.*

"Human rights" is a vital concept

Revive Our Hearts founder Nancy Leigh DeMoss[18] says,

> You'll never see a sign that says, "You have the right of way." Instead, the signs instruct us to "Yield" the right of way. That is how traffic flows best; it is also how life works best.[19]

But it seems that Nancy has failed to consider that while one driver is "yielding" in traffic, the other driver is going forward. If both of them only yielded, neither of them would ever get anywhere. Instead, both of

---

[17] At the A Cry for Justice website, www.cryingoutforjustice.com, abuse is defined: "A pattern of coercive control (ongoing actions or inactions) that proceeds from a mentality of entitlement to power, whereby, through intimidation, manipulation and isolation, the abuser keeps his [or her] target subordinated and under his control. This pattern can be emotional, verbal, psychological, spiritual, sexual, financial, social and/or physical."

[18] Now Nancy DeMoss Wolgemuth.

[19] DeMoss, *Lies Women Believe,* p 74.

them are following the rules of the road they had to know before they could pass their driver's tests. They're both abiding by *what is right*. This is why it's called the "*right* of way."

– What are "rights"?

When we're talking about what a word means, it's always good to look at the actual definition. In this case, there are at least a dozen pertinent definitions. In Webster's 1828 dictionary, one is "Conformity to the will of God, or to his law, the perfect standard of truth and justice."[20] Another refers to abiding by human laws. Another, to doing justice. All of them are about "what is right."

But it's important to see that these definitions are interconnected with the other definitions about *rights*, like this one: "That which justly belongs to one." Or this one: "Just claim by courtesy, customs, or the principles of civility and decorum."[21] For that definition, Webster decided to give the sample sentence, "Every man has a *right* to civil treatment."[22] Five more definitions expand on the concept of "rights."

So you see the interconnection? You have human and civil *rights* because it is *right* to have them.

You may have been involved in teaching children, even toddlers, about the *right* way to treat others. This is because other people have legitimate *rights*. If you were to teach one child to "give up his rights" to the other child, you know this would open the door for bullying.

The same is true in the Christian community.

If "the things that make us angry are [violations of] personal rights,"[23] it is simply because God has built into each one of us a natural justice system—a natural sense of *what is right*. It will be flawed, it will need to

---

[20] Noah Webster, *American Dictionary of the English Language*, 1828 Facsimile Edition (Foundation for American Christian Education, 1967), definition of *right*.

[21] Ibid.

[22] I hope he meant women too!

[23] Bill Gothard, "Basic Seminar Session 8: How to Transform Irritations," Embassy Media video, www.embassymedia.com.

be trained as to what is truly right, but justice, or a sense of rightness, is given by God.

When William Wilberforce spoke out tirelessly for decades for the slaves to be freed, it was because he believed they had basic human rights.

Stripping you of human rights
can be seen as an effort to strip you of humanity.

– Our nation was founded on "human rights"

Several of the authors I read used scare quotes for the word "rights," as if they wanted to demean and belittle the concept of personal rights. But one of them, in a momentary turnabout, says, "Jefferson got one thing right which was that rights come from the Creator."[24]

That's true. That's why they're called *inalienable*—human rights are rights that can't be taken away. They seemed so natural that the Founding Fathers even called them "natural law."

Natural Law can be boiled down to two parts: 1. Do not encroach on others or their property (the basis of criminal law), and 2. Do all you have agreed to do (the basis of civil law).[25]

Anything that oversteps these laws has,
in our nation and in any free society,
been considered a violation of the rights of another.

---

[24] Dan Leningen, "My 'Rights,'" Grace and Truth Bible Church, April 11, 2014. In reference to the U.S. Constitution's Bill of Rights, Leningen says, *"By demand of the people and declaration of the government,* we have the right to speak freely, have guns, write our thoughts, assemble peacefully, and follow any religion." (Italics added.) But Dan is missing some basic American history—Patrick Henry insisted on having a Bill of Rights as a hedge against a government that he believed was trying to amass too much power, believing that *inalienable rights* should be clearly stated.

[25] Richard J. Maybury, *Whatever Happened to Justice?* (Bluestocking Press, 2004), p 36.

So how does that work out in practice? Because you have rights, then if someone encroaches on you or your property, your rights have been violated. If the violation is severe enough, it's a crime.

In a wise and just society, under ordinary circumstances, that violator of your rights will be punished. One of the ways he could be punished would be by at least temporarily forfeiting some of his own rights—for example, his right to freedom of movement, since he'll be incarcerated.

Our Founders knew that if people can violate individual rights and get away with it, the structure of families, communities, and even the whole society would be damaged. They knew that the way for power grabbers to be kept in check was by the recognition and exercise of *individual rights*.

Can you imagine the Founding Fathers being told that they should yield their rights or surrender their rights or live as if they had no rights? Basic human and civil rights were what they lived and died for. This is a foundational belief on which this nation was built.

But an even more important question is, does the Bible teach it? And the answer is *yes*.

– Human rights in the Bible

The last six of the Ten Commandments—the laws regarding human interactions—unmistakably imply human rights.
- *Do not kill* implies the right to life.
- *Do not commit adultery* implies the right to spousal faithfulness.
- *Do not steal* and *do not covet* imply the right to property.
- *Do not bear false witness* implies the right to an honest presentation of one's reputation.

---

*And since being right and doing right and having rights
are all interrelated,
the concept of human rights
is inseparable from the concept of justice.*

> *Proverbs 31:8-9*
> *Open your mouth for the mute,*
> *for the **rights** of all who are destitute.*
> *Open your mouth, **judge righteously**,*
> *defend the **rights** of the poor and needy.*

> *Isaiah 1:17*
> *Learn to do good; seek **justice**, correct oppression;*
> *bring **justice** to the fatherless, plead the widow's cause.*

> *Micah 6:8*
> *He has told you, O man, what is good;*
> *and what does the Lord require of you but to do **justice**,*
> *and to love kindness, and to walk humbly with your God?*

> *Psalm 82:3*
> *Give **justice** to the weak and the fatherless;*
> *maintain the **right** of the afflicted and the destitute.*

The destitute, the poor, the needy, the weak, the fatherless, the widow, all of them have rights. Others who love God are called to help them maintain their rights.

In Luke 18, Jesus told a story about the widow who went before the unjust judge. She sought justice for herself, apparently because she believed she had rights—probably based on Scriptures like these.

During the time when Jesus lived on earth, the Pharisees severely afflicted the poor and needy, especially the widows. But Jesus didn't say anything to those widows about yielding their rights. Instead, in Luke 3:7 our Just Judge echoed the words of John the Baptist, who warned those abusers, the Pharisees, "Brood of vipers! Who has warned you to flee from the wrath to come?"

And what did he say about the children?

> *Whosoever shall offend one of these little ones that believe in me, it is better for him that a millstone were hanged about his neck, and he were cast into the sea.*[26]

God will hold accountable those who violate the rights of the little ones, leading them astray.

So the Bible definitely teaches human rights. But what about the life of Christ? One of the ways "yield your rights" teachers often present their teaching is through the life of Jesus—they say Jesus yielded His rights.

But the Bible shows otherwise . . .

– Jesus always retained His rights

If you've ever read *The Prince and the Pauper* by Mark Twain, you'll remember that Prince Edward is curious to discover what it would be like to live as a commoner. But even when he steps into the role of "pauper," he knows full well that he still retains all the rights and privileges of the king's son.

The story is complicated by the fact that Tom Canty, a boy who looks just like Edward, has taken his place, so people don't believe Edward is the prince (and eventually, the king), but once the truth is revealed, Edward steps back into the position and role that *all along have been rightfully his.* Even though he has lived as a pauper, never for a moment did he yield his rights as royalty.

The same is true for Jesus.

---

*When Jesus came to earth to live among us,
accomplishing His mission on earth to do the Father's will,
He always retained His rights as the Son of God.
Though people didn't believe Him,
all along the position and role were rightfully His.*

---

[26] Mark 9:42, KJV.

In Matthew 5:39, Jesus taught, "But I say to you, Do not resist the one who is evil. But if anyone slaps you on the right cheek, turn to him the other also." Some have taught that Jesus here is teaching the giving up of rights.

But Jesus Himself was slapped on His cheek, and the whole scene is played out for us in the gospels. This is the account in John 18:22-23.

> *When he had said these things, one of the officers standing by struck Jesus with his hand, saying, "Is that how you answer the high priest?" Jesus answered him, "If what I said is wrong, bear witness about the wrong; but if what I said is right, why do you strike me?"*

Jesus defended Himself—as being right. If we take the "turning the other cheek" exhortation at face value, it seems that He didn't obey His own orders.

But the "slapping on the cheek" Jesus referred to in Matthew 5:39 wasn't a violent punch intended to inflict pain. It was a slap intended to show contempt—in those days, it was a common way of humiliating a person.[27] Turning the other cheek would actually show self-respect, as if to silently say, "I will not respond in kind. I will show this man I am a person of dignity, every bit his equal." When Jesus spoke to the officer who struck Him across the face, He spoke in a similar way. Essentially He was saying, "If I deserved this slap, then show Me how I did. If I didn't deserve it, *then you were not right to give it to Me.*"

But Jesus isn't the only example people name when they talk about giving up rights. They also talk about Paul.

---

[27] "To strike a person on the right cheek implied giving someone the back of the hand from a right-handed person. It is not so much the hurt as the insult that is here in mind, because it was a symbolic way of insulting a person's honor." Clinton Arnold, general editor, *Zondervan Illustrated Bible Backgrounds Commentary* (Zondervan, 2002), Volume I, p 104.

– Paul's claim on his rights as a citizen

Ancient Rome was considered an advanced civilization partly because of the rights its citizens enjoyed. One of those citizens was the apostle Paul.

There was a time when Paul was about to be flogged unjustly. If he had "yielded" all his rights, he wouldn't have spoken up about that injustice at all. Instead, he did speak up. Here is the story, from Acts 22:24-29.

> *The tribune ordered [Paul] to be brought into the barracks, saying that he should be examined by flogging, to find out why they were shouting against him like this. But when they had stretched him out for the whips, Paul said to the centurion who was standing by, "Is it lawful for you to flog a man who is a Roman citizen and uncondemned?"*
>
> *When the centurion heard this, he went to the tribune and said to him, "What are you about to do? For this man is a Roman citizen." So the tribune came and said to him, "Tell me, are you a Roman citizen?" And he said, "Yes." The tribune answered, "I bought this citizenship for a large sum." Paul said, "But I am a citizen by birth."*
>
> *So those who were about to examine him withdrew from him immediately, and the tribune also was afraid, for he realized that Paul was a Roman citizen and that he had bound him.*

Though Paul didn't always make use of his legitimate rights like this,[28] he shows here that he never yielded the right to claim his citizenship. As a result, he avoided an undeserved flogging.[29]

---

*If we follow Paul's example,
we can speak up for our rights.*

---

[28] Examined more on page 24.

[29] This violation of Paul's rights was being conducted by a Roman soldier, a person who could actually get in trouble for violating them. The other people who persecuted Paul, mostly Jews who hated Jesus Christ, didn't care about his rights and were very willing to violate them.

Other Scriptures that address the idea of rights

What about Scriptures like Luke 6:22-23?

Blessed are you when people hate you and when they exclude you and revile you and spurn your name as evil, on account of the Son of Man! Rejoice in that day, and leap for joy, for behold, your reward is great in heaven; for so their fathers did to the prophets.

Or what about Hebrews 10:34?

[Y]ou joyfully accepted the plundering of your property, since you knew that you yourselves had a better possession and an abiding one.

Aren't those examples of believers who "yielded their rights"?
Not really. Instead . . .

– Scriptures showing human or civil rights can be violated

Notice something about the property belonging to the Christians that was plundered in Hebrews 10:34. It was *still theirs*.

The Hebrew Christians held fast to a view of what was eternally important—as we want to do—so they were able to rejoice as their property was plundered by people who hated Jesus and His gospel.

But those who plundered their property were violating their rights. They would still answer to God for their wrongdoing.

Disciples of Jesus who are hated, excluded, and reviled for His Name are also reminded to keep that eternal view.

When we keep the eternal perspective,
we can rejoice even when our rights are violated.

But in spite of this eternal perspective, it doesn't change the fact that the people who do the hating, excluding, and reviling are doing wrong, *even if they claim to be followers of Jesus*. They are still responsible before God for their wrongdoing. Remember what Jesus said:

> *It is impossible but that offences will come:*
> *but woe unto him through whom they come!*[30]

This Scripture shows that God will call to account those who violate the rights of another.

But what about I Corinthians 9, the biggest "rights-yielding" support Scripture of all? It's important to address those . . .

– Scriptures showing we can refrain from "making use of" our rights

Paul was a man whose desires were aligned with the will of God. His greatest desire was to see the Kingdom of God come all over the world, with the salvation of Jesus Christ that frees people from sin and shame. The fire of desire burning inside him was to see this accomplished.

In I Corinthians 9 Paul explained his genuine right to be financially supported in the work of the ministry. But even though the Christians who should have supported him were too apathetic or contrary to fulfill this genuine right, he made it clear that he wouldn't let that stop him from fulfilling his great desire. In verse 12, he said,

> *Nevertheless, we have not made use of this right, but we endure anything rather than put an obstacle in the way of the gospel of Christ.*

For the sake of the gospel, Paul chose to refrain from exercising his rights. This is different from "yielding" or "surrendering" rights.

To show the difference: In the United States if you're a registered citizen over the age of 18, you have a legal right to vote. Each election cycle, you make a decision about whether or not you'll choose to exercise that right. If for some reason you decide not to vote, that doesn't mean you've "yielded" the right to vote—it's still your right. If you say you're not going to, but at the last minute change your mind and decide to go to the polls, you can still make use of this right, because it has been your right all along.

---

[30] Luke 17.1, KJV.

Paul knew what his rights were, but for the sake of the gospel, he chose not to use them. In I Corinthians 9:18, he said,

What then is my reward? That in my preaching I may present the gospel free of charge, so as not to make full use of my right in the gospel.[31]

When Prince Edward in *The Prince and the Pauper* decides to live as a pauper for a while, he wasn't giving up his rights as the king's son. He was simply deciding not to "make use of" those rights in order to fulfill his desire to experience a pauper's life.

A wife and mother may rightly claim that it is right for her husband to provide for the family, based on I Timothy 5:8, *"But if anyone does not provide for his relatives, and especially for members of his household, he has denied the faith and is worse than an unbeliever."* But just like Paul, even greater than her rightful desire to be provided for is her desire to care for her children. If the husband refuses to care for them, instead of continuing to insist that this legitimate right be fulfilled, she may do other things in order to provide for her children. This doesn't mean that she has "yielded the right" for the family to be provided for. It's still their right, and the husband and father should still fulfill it.

No matter how your rights may be violated, no matter what rights you may decide to refrain from using, those rights are still yours.

Untwisted Truth from Chapter One

- Every person God created has human rights.
- Jesus and Paul never gave up their human rights.
- Our rights can be violated.
- We can refrain from "making use of" our rights.

---

[31] At the beginning of I Corinthians chapter 9, the ESV has the heading "Paul Surrenders His Rights." I believe a more appropriate heading would be "Paul's Example as an Apostle" (Holman), "Paul's Rights as an Apostle" (NIV), or the (perhaps somewhat unwieldy) heading given by J.B. Phillips, "I am entitled to a reward, yet I have not taken it."

CHAPTER 2

So I'm not supposed to "yield my rights"?

It's important in Untwisting Scriptures not only to present the truth, but also to show what was wrong with the incorrect teaching. So let's do some more untwisting.

What are the "no-rights" teachers missing?

The give-up-your-rights teachers seem to make several fundamental mistakes. First, the truth that Chapter 1 was devoted to. . . .

– They fail to acknowledge genuine human and civil rights

According to the "yield your rights" teachers, here's how the rights issue would play out in your daily life.

Let's say you've yielded your right, for example, to choose where you're going to live, to the controlling pastor (the one mentioned on page 11) to make that decision for you.

If you've yielded that right to him, then it has become his right, and he isn't doing wrong by making that decision. In fact, he's doing right.

Right?

Or let's say you've yielded your right to your personal property. Then when your husband smashes the heirloom dishes you inherited from your grandmother, he isn't doing wrong, because they aren't yours any more.

Right?

But if those teachings are untwisted to show that you really *do* retain those rights, then that means when authorities and pseudo-authorities violate your rights, *they are doing wrong.*

I teach English as a Second Language. Once when I was subbing in a conversation class, I centered a discussion topic on the basic human right to freedom of thought. (I didn't say "freedom of religion" because "freedom of thought" was already controversial enough!)

In that class were students from several countries, including some that allow for no freedom of religion, such as Saudi Arabia. As you can imagine, the discussion was lively, with much disagreement and some people thinking new thoughts for the first time.

Saudi Arabia might be among the more repressive regimes in the world when it comes to freedom of thought. The Arabian people live under sharia law, which means they can be killed for thinking or believing contrary to what the government declares is acceptable. But most Americans would agree that sharia law violates basic human rights.

The recognition of freedom of thought was probably one of the most important contributions of our Founding Fathers to making our nation great in its establishment. And yet . . .

An individual Christian
who unquestioningly takes this no-rights teaching to heart
is in danger of having all freedom of thought
crushed by the one in authority.

One of the "yield your rights" teachers, Nancy Leigh DeMoss,[1] surprisingly mocks the U.S. Declaration of Independence when she says,

---

[1] Now Nancy DeMoss Wolgemuth.

> From the Declaration of Independence to fast-food chicken, "I've got a right" has become the watch cry of Western civilization. In our generation, this has been particularly true of women.[2]

But I believe even Nancy would want to see those "inalienable rights" extended throughout all the societies of the world, even to the women.

Another thing the "yield your rights" teachers miss is . . .

– They confuse vertical and horizontal relationships

If you've trusted Christ as your Savior, you know that all our property ultimately belongs to God, and even our very lives. This is why only God has the right to take someone's life. And so, if by sickness or storm or other "act of God," life or property is taken, even while we grieve these losses,[3] we can submit to Him and trust Him.

---

*Before God, we understand that our personal belongings—
including our bodies—really belong to Him,
and any decisions we make are to be subject to Him.*

This is the "vertical relationship," between you and God. But in "horizontal relationships," between you and others, God has given rights to each one of us. One obvious example of "horizontal rights" is those of helpless babies. God has ultimate control over his existence, but on a horizontal level, before other people, that baby has a *right to life*.

It seems, though, that in "rights-yielding" teaching, the vertical relationship often gets tangled up with horizontal relationships.

For example, Dan Leningen is referring to horizontal relationships, with other people, when he wrongly says,

---

[2] DeMoss, *Lies Women Believe*, p 73. I found it especially surprising that DeMoss belittled the Declaration, seeing as how she wrote *The Rebirth of America* (Arthur S. DeMoss Foundation, 1986), which details the development of the U.S. Declaration of Independence and Constitution, with a hefty emphasis on our God-given rights.

[3] The reality and rightness of grief is discussed in detail in Chapter 3.

> Demanding your "rights" is pride in expecting that you deserve to be treated a certain way.[4]

I wish this writer could picture himself being in the position of one of the children being trafficked in slave labor in Africa. Or of one of the sex trafficking victims here in the United States or around the world. I hope he might then realize it isn't pride to expect a right to be treated with justice and integrity, but simply a matter of human dignity, as a being made in the image of God.

In one of the most troubling statements I mentioned earlier, the Institute in Basic Life Principles says regarding horizontal relationships,

> Just because you are alive, you probably believe you have the right to be accepted as an individual, to express opinions, to earn and spend a living, to control your personal belongings, and to make decisions. You expect others to respect your rights.[5]

Certainly you should expect others to respect rights like these. If you find that you're living without the right to be accepted as an individual or the right to express your opinion, if you find that someone else is exercising control over your personal decisions, then you'll find that you're living under a totalitarian regime, even if it is being mislabeled as a Christian marriage, a willing submission, a loyal following, or "protecting the cause of Christ."

And finally, a very important problem in the "no-rights" teaching . . .

– *They fail to distinguish rights from desires*

If I were to drive through a red light, the police officer isn't going to tell me to surrender my right to go through the red light. He'll tell me it

---

[4] Dan Leningen, "My 'Rights.'"
[5] "What is the principle of ownership?" Institute in Basic Life Principles. www.iblp.org/questions/what-principle-ownership.

wasn't right. I can't "surrender" it, because it never was my right in the first place, even if I may have thought or felt like it was.

I might imagine that I have other rights too. I might think I have a right to "avoid reaping what I sow," "defy authority," or "have other people meet all my needs."[6]

But it's not helpful to tell me to "surrender" those non-rights. Instead, you need to tell me they aren't my rights in the first place!

In one of the quotations I cited earlier, Nancy Leigh DeMoss says,

> All too often, I find myself annoyed and perturbed when things don't go my way. A decision someone makes at the office, a rude driver on the freeway, a long line at the checkout counter, a thoughtless word spoken by a family member, a minor offense (real or perceived) by a friend, someone who fails to come through on a commitment, a phone call that wakes me when I have just fallen off to sleep—if I am staking out my rights, even the smallest violation of those rights can leave me feeling and acting moody, uptight, and angry.[7]

Nancy talks about "wanting things to go my way." But that's not *rights*. That's *desires*. The relatively insignificant desires she names were never her rights to begin with. And she never even tries to grapple with the issue of huge offenses, of real human rights. If she were to distinguish between desires and genuine rights, she could give much more valuable help to her significant readership.

Hope for the Heart founder June Hunt says,

> But what are our legitimate rights? One person would answer, "Happiness." Another would say, "Freedom to live life my way."[8]

But again, these aren't really rights at all—they're only desires. Thinking that these are rights doesn't make them so. And again, June doesn't

---

[6] Grace Life International, "Handout 13: Surrendering Rights," www.gracelifeinternational.com/category/surrendering-rights. On the handout, no distinction was made between real rights and imagined rights.

[7] Nancy Leigh DeMoss, *Lies Women Believe*, p 76.

[8] June Hunt, *Anger: Facing the Fire Within* (Rose Publishing, 2013), p 44.

talk about real human rights, such as life, liberty, and equitable, just treatment.

In fact, in all the books, blogs, and lectures I read and listened to regarding yielding rights, I found only one writer who actually allowed for genuine rights that should be retained:

> There are certain areas you should not lay down your rights. You do have a right to a safe home, and so in an abusive situation, you need to get help. When it comes to society, you do have the right to speak up against injustice. . . . [9]

If more teachers focused on distinguishing the difference between desires and genuine rights, we could go a long way—not only in guiding believers in their spiritual growth, but also in getting help to people in desperate need whose basic human and civil rights are being violated or taken from them.

The "no-rights" teachers also have the problem of "proof-texting" or *eisegesis*.[10]

– They twist Scriptures to teach their "no rights" doctrine

The people who teach that you should yield your rights will reference several Scriptures in support of their teachings. But they assume ideas that simply aren't in the texts. Here's an example:

---

[9] Karol Ladd, *A Woman's Passionate Pursuit of God* (Harvest House, 2011), p 84.

[10] *Eisegesis* is a coined word (derived from the word *exegesis*), meaning "to read into," (since the Greek prefix *eis-* means "into" and *ex-* means "out of"). People who practice eisegesis come to the Bible with their minds already made up about what it should say, and then look for proof texts to back up their pre-formed decisions. The earliest use of the word I could find was from 1873: "He [the minister] should be correct in things little as well as great; should practice *ex*egesis rather than *eis*egesis. Careful laymen have said of more than one minister: 'He makes his own texts.'" Prof. Edwards A. Park, "The Structure of a Sermon—the Text," *Bibliotheca Sacra and Theological Review*, (Andover Theological Seminary), Volume 30, p 562.

> Philippians 2:5 says we're told to let this mind be in you which was in Christ Jesus, who being in the very form of God *did not cling to his rights as God's equal*, but *He stripped Himself of all of His rights* and consented to become a slave and lived a life of total obedience even to the extent of dying on the cross. And He did that to demonstrate to you and me what our mental attitude ought to be.[11]

If you read that actual passage of Scripture, you'll find that it is being misrepresented. Instead,

When Christ came to earth,
He did many things to accomplish the Father's will.
But He always retained all His rights as the rightful Son of God.

There are many teachings that say Jesus gave up His rights. Another one says,

> Jesus yielded His right to make His own decisions. Perhaps the most difficult right to yield is that of making final decisions. Yet, if we do not fully yield this right to God, we will not develop a spirit of meekness or walk in true humility before God. Jesus lived in complete surrender to God's direction.[12]

This article gives two examples of Christ's "yielding His rights to make His own decisions." First, it says that Jesus as a child yielded Himself in obedience to His earthly parents.

But think about this: even in Jesus' childhood, the will of the Father always came first. If the Father's will had ever conflicted with the will of his parents, Jesus would have followed His Father's will, because that's what He came to earth to accomplish.

---

[11] Bill Gothard, "Basic Seminar Session 8: How to Transform Irritations," www.embassymedia.com. Italics added.

[12] "Did Jesus Christ yield personal rights?" Institute in Basic Life Principles. www.iblp.org/questions/did-jesus-christ-yield-personal-rights.

In fact, there actually *was* a time when the Father's will conflicted with the will of His parents. When Jesus was twelve years old He went missing, and His earthly parents hunted for Him for three days. When they finally found Him and His mother rebuked Him, Jesus rebuked her right back, recorded in Luke 2:49. *"Why were you looking for me? Did you not know that I must be in my Father's house?"*

Even as a child, Jesus retained His rights as the Son of God, accomplishing His mission on earth to do the Father's will.

In the article mentioned above, the second example of Christ's "yielding His right to make His own decisions" is Jesus as an adult yielding Himself to God the Father.

Well, yes, He did that. Of course Jesus always accomplished the Father's will perfectly. But the article fails to say anything about the adult Jesus yielding His rights to any people. Because He *didn't*.

In fact, Jesus emphatically stated in John 10:18,

No one takes [my life] from me, but I lay it down of my own accord. I have authority to lay it down, and I have authority to take it up again. This charge I have received from my Father.

This is so important to see. Jesus always lived in perfect accord with the Father's will. But as far as His rights are concerned—both His divine rights and His human rights—He yielded them to no one on this earth. He retained His full authority throughout His life.

---

*If we want to be like Jesus,
we will desire to do the Father's will
even while we retain our legitimate rights.*

The Love Dare Day by Day: A Year of Devotions for Couples entitles one section "Love lays down its rights."[13] One of the support Scriptures is John 5:39, *"My judgment is righteous, because I do not seek My own will, but*

---

[13] Stephen Kendrick and Alex Kendrick, *The Love Dare Day by Day: A Year of Devotions for Couples* (B&H Books, 2013), p 37.

the will of Him who sent Me." Another is Matthew 26:36-42, in which Jesus prayed in the garden, *"Not My will, but Thine be done."*

Again, we can make the same observation: the mission of Jesus was to do the Father's will, which He accomplished as the "rightful" Son of God.

In a blog post entitled "Give Up Your Rights" on the church website of Fellowship Memphis,[14] popular speaker and author Bryan Loritts wrote, "Jesus . . . had the right to come off the cross. After all he was being executed unjustly. . . . Jesus could have called legions of angels to come [take Him] off the cross. I believe he had that right."

So far, I can agree with Loritts. It's refreshing to see someone say that Jesus actually had rights.

But then he goes on to say,

> But the beauty of the cross, and therefore the beauty of the gospel, is that Jesus *laid down his rights*, died, that we might live![15]

Actually, as the rightful Son of God, Jesus retained that right to call those legions of angels, up to the very end. He did not make use of His rights because of His greater purpose, His rights were violated, and the people who called for His death had blood on their hands.[16]

---

[14] Fellowship Memphis is in the Acts 29 family of church-planting churches founded by Mark Driscoll of the former Mars Hill Church and Matt Chandler of the Village Church.

[15] Bryan Crawford Loritts, "Give Up Your Rights," Fellowship Memphis. www.fellowshipmemphis.org/bryanloritts/?p=77, accessed September 20, 2014. Italics added. This post was removed from the church website sometime after Bryan left the church, which was sometime after he was allegedly involved in covering up sex crimes in the church. The following article tells how the leaders of Fellowship Memphis, one of whom was Loritts, allegedly discouraged the victims, some of whom were underage, from reporting to the police. Could it be that the church leaders thought the victims should give up their rights? David Waters, "Churches tried to help Trotter; what about victims?" August 13, 2016, www.commercialappeal.com.

[16] Matthew 23:32-36.

Many no-rights advocates use Jonah as an example of a person who sinfully insisted on his rights instead of yielding them. But if you read the book of Jonah, you'll find that twice the Lord said to him, "Do you do well to be angry?"[17] This question indicated that Jonah's anger was not "right," which means it wasn't his right to feel that way. In wanting the Ninevites to be destroyed, Jonah was feeling a desire, not a right.

In Dan Leningen's blog post cited earlier, he says,

> As Christians we are called to give up a right to our life [in order] to serve God and others (Matt. 10:39;16:25; Mark 8:35; Luke 9:24; 17:33; John 12:25).[18]

All six of these references repeat the same truth: If you try to save your life (by turning from Christ) you will lose it, but if you're willing to lose your life (by following Christ), you will save it. Here is one of them, Matthew 10:39: *"Whoever finds his life will lose it, and whoever loses his life for my sake will find it."*

Christ calls you to follow Him, which will look like "losing your life" (your temporal desires and preferences) in the eyes of the world. But even then, you have basic human rights that are yours because you are made in the image of God.

As you follow Him, your rights may be violated.
But they are still your rights, because you are made in His image.

As far as I could find, the teaching that Christians should "yield their rights" began to be taught and circulated in our churches and Christian communities sometime after World War II. Apparently the proof texts that have been used to support it in the past few decades hadn't been noticed before that time.

---

[17] Jonah chapter 4.
[18] Dan Leningen, "My 'Rights.'"

Perhaps the biggest problem that results from the no-rights teaching is . . .

Double standards are created

After about fifty or sixty years of the no-rights teaching in our churches, we can see the way it has played out and the two different double standards that have become obvious.

– The "no-rights" doctrine applies only to certain rights, not others

You're taught that you should give up your rights, and you try to put it into practice. You don't stand up for yourself or speak about any "real or perceived" violations against yourself.

But it seems that there are certain times this rule doesn't apply.

What about murder? Can you imagine your pastor not reporting the murder of a beloved family member because he or she had "yielded all rights"?

What about reporting large-scale theft, such as that of a car? Your pastor could decide to overlook it, but if he reported it to the police, would he be doing wrong, because he should have "given up his rights" to that car? I think no one would agree with that. After all, living in a free society means those who violate certain rights of others are caught and punished.

What about rights violations by the government, against us? Many of the same people who will tell you to give up your rights will also speak out when certain of our rights as U.S. citizens are violated.

One more thing . . . I read a whole lot of books and websites that tell us to yield our rights or surrender our rights or give up or lay down our rights. Every time, I kept coming across this statement on what's called the "copyright" page (or post): *All rights reserved.* These teachers who claim that we should all lay down our rights, what are they saying with a statement like that one?

– The "no-rights" doctrine applies only to certain people, not others

Again, you're taught you should give up your rights, and you try to put it into practice. You don't stand up for yourself or speak about any "real or perceived" violations against yourself.

But it seems that there are certain people in the Christian community to whom this rule doesn't apply.

As it turns out, the ones without rights are the ones "under authority." Those who are in positions of authority, and those in positions of power and influence . . . well, they always seem to retain their rights.

After all, if one person is "yielding," the other is going forward.
As one is giving up rights, the other is taking them.

If, for example, you're being told you need to give up your right to make decisions, then someone else is going to retain the right to make those decisions for you.

Sometimes it can take years to see this double standard. There can be several reasons for this—maybe you were raised with the teaching, or maybe you were a new Christian when you came into it, and just wanted to do everything right. Maybe you were afraid.

But if a respected man in the church community abuses someone, and others with "authority" gather to protect the abuser, those in authority will most surely use a variety of tactics on the victim to get him or her to be silenced. One commonly used tactic is this one: "You need to yield your rights. Christians should have no rights." With this command, the powerful are protected, and the vulnerable are crushed and confused.

This is not the heart of God.
Rather, this is a noxious stink in the nostrils of God.

So there's got to be a new way of thinking.

Instead of thinking about "yielding rights"...

– We want our desires to be aligned with God's will

Psalm 37:4 says, *"Delight yourself in the LORD, and he will give you the desires of your heart."* As you find your joy in God, by faith, He will give you the desires that will correspond with His will.

How does that work out in practice?

Suppose you're exhorted to surrender your right to "have visible security."[19] But instead of thinking about "rights," you'll think about your desires and His will.

So you can say, "Lord, my desire is to have visible security. Is this just because I want to live in comfort, or is it because I want to do what You've called me to do?" You may be called as a missionary to a dangerous culture, in which case you can trust the Lord to work in you to change your desire, to be willing and even glad to trust Him in living without visible security.

Or on the other hand, you and your children may be living in terror of an abusive spouse, in which case you may see that, far from having "no right" to visible security, you have a responsibility to protect yourself and your children.

Perhaps you're exhorted to surrender your rights to "be accepted by others," or "have a good reputation."[20]

Instead you can say, "Lord, my desire is to have a good reputation. Why do I want that? Is it because I want to exalt myself, or is it because I want to do what You've called me to do?" You may be maligned because you speak out for the Lord in a culture that mocks Him, and in that case He can give you joy in the face of that persecution.

---

[19] Grace Life International, "Handout 13: Surrendering Rights," www.gracelifeinternational.com/category/surrendering-rights.

[20] Ibid. Assuming, of course, that your character is worthy of a good reputation. If your character is wicked, then *you have no right* to a good reputation.

Or on the other hand, you may be living with a spouse who spreads lies about you, defaming you to others, in which case the Lord may be calling you to get out and to speak out, with dignity and grace.

As you seek the Lord, you can ask Him to remove from your heart any desires He doesn't want you to have. You can ask Him to strengthen your desires for things He does want you to have, and show you why you should have them, trusting in Him as a good God who loves you and wants the best for you.

> *Taking your desires before the Lord*
> *to align them with His will*
> *is a way of walking by faith.*
> *It is living the Christian life actively instead of passively.*

One of the many examples I read of rights you "should be willing to give up" is the right to a good night's sleep if your child is sick. But it can get confusing thinking about your child's "right" for help, and trying to sort it out from your own "right" to sleep. Which person is supposed to "yield their rights"?

Instead, you can reject this thinking about rights at all, and think about aligning your desires with God's will. You can think about how the Lord wants you, the caregiver and protector, to love and protect those in your care. He may well want you to put a cool cloth on a hot forehead and hold a small hand and sing a quiet song, even as your own head is nodding off to sleep.

I thought of a different situation, though, when I heard Bill Gothard say

> If you give God your right to a good night's sleep, and then something awakens you tonight halfway through the night, you thank God for a half night's sleep.[21]

---

[21] Bill Gothard, "Basic Seminar Session 8," www.embassymedia.com.

Instead of thinking about a sick child, I thought of a friend who was married to a man who woke her up throughout the night, night after night, for various forms of intimate interaction, so she couldn't get the sleep she needed.

If she thinks she needs to "yield her rights" to a good night's sleep, she won't say anything about this significant problem. But if she understands that she doesn't need to fear disobeying God in not "yielding her rights" to her husband in his demands, this will be an important step in discerning the right thing to do in this situation, another one in which the stronger one should be loving and protecting.

If you've lived under ongoing spiritual abuse, it may take time and good counsel to sort out the voice of the Lord from the voice of the abuser. But one thing you can know for sure: your genuine rights (human and civil) are yours, and it's wrong for others to violate them.

When it comes to your desires, you don't need to ignore them, the way the no-rights teachers would have you think. Instead you can bring your desires before the Lord, to ask Him to help your desires align with His will. The closer you grow to Him, the more in tune the two will be.

> *Aligning our desires with God's will*
> *is an important part of the process, the journey,*
> *of growth in Christ.*
> *But it's done by faith, step by step,*
> *looking to Him every step of the way*
> *to make the next step clear.*

This leads to another important point . . .

– We want to live the Christian life by faith, not works

One thing that deeply troubles me about the rights-yielding teaching is that many of the teachers take it so far that they end up proclaiming it as a gospel of works.

> So that the very essence of the gospel is the dying of self, and the laying down of rights.[22]

But the essence of the gospel is not dying to self or laying down rights. Galatians 3:1-3 refutes this teaching:

> *O foolish Galatians! Who has bewitched you? It was before your eyes that Jesus Christ was publicly portrayed as crucified. Let me ask you only this: Did you receive the Spirit by works of the law or by hearing with faith? Are you so foolish? Having begun by the Spirit, are you now being perfected by the flesh?*

Instead, the *only* essence of the gospel is the full salvation of Jesus Christ by His bloody death for the penalty of sin and His victorious resurrection over the power of sin and shame, by which we too can live and walk in victory, *by faith*.

The essence of the gospel
includes Christ's ascension into the heavenlies
and His seating at the right hand of God the Father,
which through Him
are our right and privileges as well, by faith.

Another writer has said,

> Only when you release your rights will you have the mind of Christ, be able to walk in the Spirit, and see His fruit produced in your life.[23]

This is a false teaching. Instead, Christ calls you to live by faith and walk in faith, in the power of the Spirit, not by striving and struggling to do more and be more (or as the case may be, do less and be less), but by

---

[22] Bryan Crawford Loritts, "Give Up Your Rights," Fellowship Memphis, www.fellowshipmemphis.org/bryanloritts/?p=77, accessed September 20, 2014.

[23] Dan Leningen, "My 'Rights,'" Grace and Truth Bible Church, April 11, 2014. www.gtbchurch.org/posts/18778.

trusting the One who has fulfilled all your righteousness for you that He has promised He will empower you to "work out" by His "working in."[24]

This is genuinely good news.

But there's more good news. There is something truly beautiful that it seems almost all of the no-rights teachers have missed.

Christians have specific rights in Christ

You wouldn't hear a whole lot about these rights in many Christian circles. When they tell us to give up our rights, most of them don't make any distinctions.

But the truth is that these rights in Christ are part of our full inheritance[25] in Him. Believing that these are *right* for us to accept and claim as believers in Christ is part of living in the fullness God has called us to.

Philippians 3:20 tells you that you are a citizen of the heavenly community. Just like the citizens of Rome (of which Paul was one) . . .

The citizens of the heavenly community
have certain important rights through Jesus Christ.

Here's one: If you're a believer in Jesus Christ, you used to be in the domain of darkness, but now you have been delivered from it and transferred into the kingdom of the Father's beloved Son.[26] Then, when you come into the kingdom of Jesus Christ, you come in not as a slave, but as a son or daughter, with all the inheritance of fully invested children of God (Colossians 1:12; Galatians 3:26 and 4:7). In fact, Paul prayed in Ephesians 1:18 that the Ephesians would have their spiritual eyes opened to see the riches of His glorious inheritance in the saints.

And because you are in Christ, fully invested as a son or daughter, you know what you have a right to do?

---

[24] Philippians 2:12-13.
[25] The importance of our inheritance is discussed more in Chapter 4.
[26] Colossians 1:13.

> *You have a right to go boldly into the holy of holies,*
> *where the curtain has been torn down,*
> *to present your case before God, knowing that, because of Christ,*
> *you can be confident of finding mercy and grace.*

Why? Because, in Christ, *it will be right for you to receive it.* This means it is *your right.*

If someone were to encourage me to claim my full inheritance in Christ, the spiritual power, the confidence in prayer that can be mine, living as if I am a fully invested daughter of the King of Kings, what if I were to reply by saying, "No, I've yielded those rights"?

That's far from the Christian life God wants me to live. He wants me to walk in the power of the Spirit, in the fullness of all He has to offer me. *That is right.*

Looking at our rights in a new light

Your rights may be violated by wicked people[27]—but those rights are still intact, and our just Judge is watching and will bring all to account.

If justice isn't served here on earth the way it should be, it will still be served. We beseech a just and good God for truth, justice, and light, and we encourage one another that He will ultimately do right.

There is a far greater way of joy than the false one of "yielding your rights."

> *As citizens together of that heavenly community,*
> *Christ-followers will have that desire to love each other,*
> *help each other, encourage each other, respect each other,*
> *and work together to give out the good news*
> *of the Kingdom of God,*
> *through our victorious Savior, Jesus Christ.*

---

[27] And sadly, wicked people are not just "out there" in the world; they are also within the church, even sometimes in leadership positions.

When our Savior, our Lord Jesus, saved us, He didn't send us out as a nameless, faceless work force, stripped of rights and identity. He knows and loves each one of us intimately. As one abuse survivor said,

> The Bible uses loving, relational word pictures: He made us His children—sons and co-heirs with Christ. He even speaks of us as His Bride, treasured before the dawn of time, loved, pursued, bought with an inestimable price. Even now Jesus is preparing a home for His Bride, planning to return for a much-anticipated reunion celebrated with a sumptuous feast and a loving eternity.

Then she added, in regard to her own words,

> I look at those words and can recognize the theological soundness of them, but I'm just now beginning to grasp a fraction of what they mean. This is just beginning to untwist for me.[28]

I pray for you, as well as many others, that the Scriptures will continue to be untwisted, to shine forth in all the beauty of the Loving and Living Word of God, Jesus Christ.

Untwisted Truth from Chapter Two

- Human rights need to be distinguished from God's ultimate authority.
- Rights need to be distinguished from desires.
- We want our desires to be aligned with God's will.
- We want to live the Christian life by faith, not works.
- Christians have specific and beautiful rights through Jesus Christ.

---

[28] Personal correspondence, used by permission.

CHAPTER 3

I still feel the effects of the pain, so "I must be bitter"

Have you been accused of being bitter?

Could it be possible to be bitter without being in sin?

What does sinful bitterness look like?

In many sermons, Christian books, and blogs, it seems that if you're not happy, you must be bitter. And bitterness appears to have only one definition: deep-seated anger, hostility, resentment, and grudge-holding against an offender (real or imagined), who has violated your rights (real or perceived). So then, they say, if you have any of these feelings, then you obviously haven't forgiven the offender, and you're in danger of not being forgiven by God.

But their teachings don't match with the teachings of the Bible as a whole. And the wrong people end up getting the blame.

"Woe to those who call evil good and good evil, who put darkness for light and light for darkness, who put bitter for sweet and sweet for bitter!"
Isaiah 5:20

How Biblical "bitterness" is often preached

As I listened to many sermons and read a number of blogs and Christian books that referenced bitterness, I began to see patterns emerge—patterns that didn't necessarily fit with Scripture.

— *They tell stories*

Storytelling carries much emotional impact—listeners often remember the stories better than they do the main part of the sermon. And bitterness seems to be a very useful topic for stories.

Bill Gothard told several stories: a man was bitter about having to pay alimony to his wife; a man was bitter because his wife had been unfaithful; a man was bitter against his father, so he ended up being like his father; and a woman was bitter because her daughter had been murdered by her husband.[1]

Bob Jones III told several stories: a man who asked for help had the problem of bitterness; a pastor who ran off with his secretary had the problem of bitterness; a friend of his whose son was killed became angry at God and couldn't get the grace of God; a girl was angry at her former boyfriend for wanting to date other girls; a man was angry with him for years because of something that had happened decades earlier.[2]

Paul Tautges told a powerful personal story about being swindled out of a large amount of money, harboring resentment toward his offenders, then forgiving and extending love to his offenders, and finally experiencing closure through a sincere repentance on the part of one of them.[3]

Bob Wood told a lengthy story about his trucking business in which if a truck's axle ran out of grease, a fire could start and all the cargo would be lost. "What a powerful example of what happens to us as

---

[1] Bill Gothard, "Basic Seminar Session 7: Dealing with Hurts / Keys to Forgiveness," Embassy Media, www.embassymedia.com.
[2] Bob Jones III, "Bitterness," October 2015, www.sermonaudio.com.
[3] Paul Tautges, "Bitter Root, Rotten Fruit," www.sermonaudio.com, Nov 2011.

Christians when we allow bitterness in our lives."[4] He told of how he shouldn't be bitter that other people could sing well when he couldn't; how he shouldn't be bitter that after teaching his sons golf their golfing skills surpassed his; how his granddaughter had conflicts with other children; and how Fanny Crosby, the blind hymn writer, "looked forward to heaven, not back to someone's failure."[5]

---

*Stories can be powerful convincing tools,
but they don't necessarily represent the truth.*

— They cite professionals

Quoting professionals can also be very convincing and even intimidating.

Paul Tautges quoted an unnamed doctor who said, "You'd never believe the results we see in people's bodies from bitterness."[6]

Bob Wood failed to elaborate on the cryptic statement, "Psychologists tell us the third step of bitterness is self-hate."[7]

Bill Gothard said, "Doctors inform us that most illnesses today are the result of bitterness or guilt or just lack of love.... Dentists explain to me that they get patients who complain of aching teeth [with no evidence of cavity or abscess], so they help these patients get over their anger, their bitterness, and then the muscles loosen up and they solve their aching teeth.... Doctors will also explain to us that when you get bitter, it goes directly to your bones, and there are certain bone diseases that can be directly traced to anger and bitterness."[8]

---

[4] The full meaning of this story wasn't quite clear to me, but it seemed to be indicating that if you're bitter, you'll lose everything.
[5] Bob Wood, "Bitterness," April 2010, www.sermonaudio.com.
[6] Tautges, "Bitter Root, Rotten Fruit."
[7] Wood, "Bitterness."
[8] Gothard, "Basic Seminar, Session 7."

Another interesting bit of information I discovered was that these teachers define Biblical bitterness in a way I couldn't find in the Bible.

— *They define bitterness as unforgiveness and resentment*

> Bitterness is resentful cynicism that results in an intense antagonism or hostility towards others.[9]

> Bitterness is unforgiveness gone to seed—defiling many.[10]

> The soil of bitterness is a heart that harbors hostility and does not deal with hurt by the grace of God.[11]

> It is a harsh, distasteful attitude that springs from a shortage of grace.[12]

But even when you've already forgiven, you may still be struggling. What then?

— *They say bitterness is hidden deep within an individual's heart*

> Bitterness is "a core sin,"[13] a "very subtle sin."[14]

> It is not easy to detect. Just as the waters of Marah looked fine but tasted bitter, so a person might look good but have a bitter spirit.[15]

> The root of bitterness is underground; it is easy to hide and camouflage. . . . Sometimes people say, "I know my heart, there's no bitterness in me." Truth of

---

[9] "Question: 'What does the Bible say about bitterness?'" GotQuestions.org. www.gotquestions.org/Bible-bitterness.

[10] Andy Reese and Jennifer Barnett, *Freedom Tools for Overcoming Life's Tough Problems* (Chosen Books, 2015), p 125.

[11] Adrian Rogers, "The Root of Bitterness," *Love Worth Finding*. www.oneplace.com/ministries/love-worth-finding/read/articles/root-of-bitterness-8599.html

[12] Tautges, "Bitter Root, Rotten Fruit."

[13] Paul Kingsbury, "The Characteristics of Bitterness," March 2008, www.sermonaudio.com.

[14] Paul Tautges, "Bitter Root, Rotten Fruit."

[15] Kingsbury, "The Characteristics of Bitterness."

> the matter is you don't know your heart. God's Word tells us, "The heart is deceitful above all things, and desperately wicked: who can know it?"[16]

> It is like heart disease. . . . The attack is sudden, but the symptoms haven't been sudden at all. . . . Bitterness is like the root of a tree. It starts below the surface and then it grows and grows and grows.[17]

— *They say bitterness is caused by . . .*

> *Resisting the grace of God*. All around us there are people who have serious and desperate needs. God gives each one enough grace to call upon Him in the time of his need and then receive more grace for the trials that he is experiencing. Often, however, people in trouble do not respond to the grace God gives them. The result is a root of bitterness.[18]

> If we take the latter course [resisting God and failing to receive His grace], bitterness will take root in the soil of our hearts. In time, that root will spring up and cause trouble for us and for others around us who will be affected by our unforgiving spirit.[19]

> *Discontent*. A lot of bitterness comes from thinking that you're owed something you haven't been given. . . . Much bitterness is because we don't get what we think we deserve.[20]

> *Not dealing with an old hurt*. The seed of bitterness is a hurt that is planted in someone. It may be intentional or unintentional. Someone does not mean to

---

[16] Adrian Rogers, "The Root of Bitterness." Jeremiah 17:9, which is being misused here, is worthy of its own chapter to be untwisted.

[17] Ibid.

[18] "Majoring on a Biblical Mandate," *Institute in Basic Life Principles*. www.iblp.org/news/majoring-biblical-mandate.

[19] Nancy Leigh DeMoss, *Choosing Forgiveness: Your Journey to Freedom* (Moody Publishers, 2008), p 76.

[20] Bob Jones III, "Bitterness," October 2015, www.sermonaudio.com.

> hurt you, but you were hurt. Sometimes the hurt is only imagined. No one has hurt you, but somehow you feel that someone has done something wrong to you.[21]
>
> *Lack of self-acceptance*. You can become angry about defects that don't allow you to do what you want to do. . . . We become bitter with the talents of other people.[22]
>
> *A temporal value system*. Whenever you and I are bitter, it proves that we have greed, that we're concerned more about temporal things than eternal values.[23]
>
> *Unmet expectations*. Bitterness grows in us when we fail to see the trouble and pain in our lives from God's point of view, and when our *expectations* of what life should be diverge from the *reality* of what life really is.[24]
>
> *Taking up offenses*. Some of the most bitter people I've ever met are those who were not offended but have taken up offenses for others. They are the most bitter people in the world. They are the ones who are taking up causes, and they don't have any grace to deal with it.[25]
>
> *Childhood abuse*. I've counseled people who've been bitter at God for decades because of childhood abuse.[26]

Almost without exception, people who write and speak about bitterness see it as the fountainhead of sin. . . .

---

[21] Rogers, "The Root of Bitterness."

[22] Bob Wood, "Bitterness."

[23] Bill Gothard, "Basic Seminar, Session 7."

[24] DeMoss, *Choosing Forgiveness*, p 73. Italics in original.

[25] Bill Gothard, "Basic Seminar Session 7." The concept of "taking up offenses" is discussed in Chapter 6.

[26] Tautges, "Bitter Root, Rotten Fruit."

— They say bitterness is the "root cause" of many other sins

> Moral defilement always follows bitterness. The Bible says so right here. You are defiled—bitterness is a root sin from which other sins emanate.[27]

> My friend, when you see that kind of persistent anger [of Ephesians 4:31], you're seeing the fruit of a root called bitterness.[28]

> At the risk of oversimplifying, after years of dealing with people who have 'fallen' into various types of immorality, I am convinced that sexual sin is almost invariably linked to a root of bitterness, as are many other sins and issues.[29]

> The thing I most often have to counsel young people about is bitterness.... Bitterness breeds sin.... Look at Adam's response to Eve: it was bitterness. Look at Cain's response to Abel: it was bitterness. And look at what they were driven to because they were caught up in the idea of bitterness.[30]

> When we fail to deal with hurts God's way, when we harbor resentment in our hearts, that bitterness—like an infection—will fester and work its way into our system, until ultimately we start viewing everything through the eyes of hurt—everything others do, everything that happens to us.[31]

> Most people who quit on God, when you boil it down to the core, most of them are bitter.[32]

The picture they paint is bleak. So then . . .

— What do they say is the solution?

- *They tell you to ask people who are more spiritual than you to point out the bitterness in your heart.*

---

[27] Bob Jones III, "Bitterness."
[28] Paul Kingsbury, "The Characteristics of Bitterness."
[29] Nancy Leigh DeMoss, *Choosing Forgiveness*, p 76.
[30] Bob Wood, "Bitterness."
[31] DeMoss, *Choosing Forgiveness*, p 59.
[32] Kingsbury, "The Characteristics of Bitterness."

> I'd like to beg of you, plead with you, to not listen to the voice of your own heart, which is deceitful above all things, to not listen to the whispers of the evil one that everything's ok, and to not just listen to the counsel and advice of those peers around you. But I pray that you will go before those who go before God and walk with God and you'll bare your soul before them, and they say, "My friend I perceive that you are in the gall of bitterness." Do not run away, do not become angry, but repent of your sin, root out bitterness out of your life. Bitterness is not easily detected, but bitterness will be detected first and foremost by those who have spiritual perception.[33]

- *They tell you to confess it, often as an equal or worse sin than the sin committed against you.*

> Confess your sins. That's the cure for bitterness. Are you holding bitterness toward another? Anger that you consider justified? It's not justified. Look at what Paul had done to him. Yet he said, "I exercise myself to avoid bitterness."[34]

> Daily remind yourself that your sin, which is already forgiven in Christ, is greater than anyone else's sin against you.[35]

> [W]rite to that person, "You may not even know I'm bitter toward you, but I am, and I'm sorry for these feelings against you."[36]

> A response of bitterness is never right when someone has done something wrong to you. You need to ask God to forgive you, and He will by His grace.[37]

---

[33] Kingsbury, "The Characteristics of Bitterness." "Those who have spiritual perception" often becomes "those who have authority or control over you." Also, Kingsbury is inconsistent in his application: if the hearts of those he is preaching to are all "deceitful above all things"—and I'd assume he would think the same thing about his own heart—then no one is qualified to make any judgment about anyone's "gall of bitterness," their own or anyone else's.

[34] Wood, "Bitterness." Actually, Paul never said this.

[35] Paul Tautges, "Bitter Root, Rotten Fruit."

[36] Jones, "Bitterness."

- *In addition to forgiving, they tell you to refuse to think about any offenses.*

  > Actively choose not to remember the wrongs of others. . . . Destroy lists of sins committed against you, mental lists or actual, written lists.[38]

  > If someone has wronged you, cut it down and forget it. By the grace of God, bury that hurt in the grave of God's forgetfulness.[39]

  > You need to be very careful not to take up offenses for the hurts of others. . . . Be very careful to refuse to take up an offense for someone else's hurt. That's their issue, that's their deal with God, you stay out of it. Don't let it affect your heart.[40]

- *They tell you to be like Joseph, who said, "You meant evil against me, but God meant it for good."*[41]

  > We thank God for what He is intending to accomplish through offenses.[42]

That's how bitterness is taught. Have teachings like these ever made you feel a burden of condemnation for struggles you may be having?[43]

I began this study with fresh eyes, exploring the Bible to find out what bitterness really is. I found that it isn't always sin, and when it is sin, it looks very different from what has typically been presented.

I began by studying the word in its English form and in its Hebrew and Greek forms, and then studying all the uses of the word in context. That's the best way to untwist these Twisted Scriptures.

---

[37] Adrian Rogers, "The Root of Bitterness."

[38] Paul Tautges, "Bitter Root, Rotten Fruit."

[39] Rogers, "The Root of Bitterness."

[40] Tautges, "Bitter Root, Rotten Fruit." The subject of "taking up offenses" is addressed in Chapter 6.

[41] Genesis 50:20.

[42] Bill Gothard, "Basic Seminar, Session 7."

[43] You may also be trying to make a wrong situation right, like the widow in Luke 18. "You're so bitter" can be a duct-tape-slap to seek to silence you, from people who do not want to take measures to correct the situation. More on that in Chapter 6.

What does the word *bitterness* mean?

The word *bitter* originally meant simply "irritating, unfavorably stimulating to the gustatory nerve, disagreeable to the palate, having the characteristic taste of wormwood."[44] But because bitter tastes are so often associated with poison, the word took on a greater meaning, to describe the intensity of feelings associated with suffering, misery, agony, and grief.[45] After that first definition about taste, there are three main ways the word is used in English.

Which kind of bitterness?	English definition	Observations	A distinctive name
A bitter experience, condition, or realization	causing severe pain and great suffering (having similar effects to poison)	This is something that happens to you, and is the cause of #2.	**#1 Source of Bitterness** "It's a bitter pill to swallow."
Bitter feelings resulting in mourning and lament	full of intense grief and misery	Words and feelings that are a natural, God-given, non-sinful response to #1.	**#2 Grieving Bitterness** "Peter wept bitterly."
Bitter feelings, bitter words, bitter actions	full of active hatred stinging, harsh, virulent full of intense overt hostility	In the ancient languages, hatred and anger aren't necessarily implied—only the acting out that causes agony and grief. *This kind of bitterness thus becomes #1 for another person.*	**#3 Destructive Bitterness** Evildoers "aim bitter words like arrows."

---

[44] Definition of *bitter*, *Oxford English Dictionary Online*. Oxford University Press, 2016. www.oed.com.

[45] "Anguish of mind, great mental trouble or distress." Definition of *agony* in *Oxford English Dictionary Online*. "Deep or violent sorrow, caused by loss or trouble; a keen or bitter feeling of regret for something lost, remorse for something done, or sorrow for mishap to oneself or others." Definition of *grief* in *Oxford English Dictionary Online*. (Oxford University Press, 1989). www.oed.com.

The First Two Kinds of Bitterness

These two kinds of bitterness are related. The Source of Bitterness causes the Grieving Bitterness.[46]

Sources of Bitterness in the Bible

A few Sources of Bitterness in the Bible	What was the "Bitter Pill"?
Genesis 26:34-35 When Esau was forty years old, he took Judith the daughter of Beeri the Hittite to be his wife, and Basemath the daughter of Elon the Hittite, and they made life **bitter** for Isaac and Rebekah.	Esau's choice to marry women who worshiped false gods caused grief to Isaac and Rebekah. ("Made life bitter" is translated in the KJV "were a grief of mind.")
Exodus 23:21 Pay careful attention to him and obey his voice; do not **rebel against him**, for he will not pardon your transgression, for my name is in him.	That term "rebel against him" ("provoke him" in the KJV) is literally "cause him bitterness" or grief, which might be a more accurate translation. The waywardness of His people caused grief to the heart of God.
Job 9:18 He will not let me get my breath, but fills me with **bitterness**.	The traumatic loss of his home, family members, and health caused grief to Job.
Proverbs 17:25 A foolish son is a grief to his father and **bitterness** to her who bore him.	When parents know that their son's foolishness will lead him to destruction, this is a cause of great agony and grief for them.

---

[46] Destructive Bitterness (#3) will be discussed in the next two chapters.

Jeremiah 2:19 Your evil will chastise you, and your apostasy will reprove you. Know and see that it is evil and **bitter** for you to forsake the LORD your God; the fear of me is not in you, declares the Lord God of hosts.	The choice to forsake the Lord will be a choice of destruction, causing agony and grief.
Jeremiah 4:18 Your ways and your deeds have brought this upon you. This is your doom, and it is **bitter**; it has reached your very heart.	The people's destructive choices have brought them destruction. This is a source of agony and grief to them.
Lamentations 1:4 The roads to Zion mourn, for none come to the festival; her gates are desolate; her priests groan; her virgins have been afflicted, and she herself suffers **bitterly**.	The people of Jeremiah's time experienced the grief of their homeland's destruction because of their sin against the Lord.
Lam 3:19 Remember my affliction and my wanderings, the **wormwood and the gall!**	Since gall (poison—in some cases the Hebrew word is translated "venom") and wormwood (a terrible tasting plant) were both very bitter, they were used metaphorically to express bitterness of soul (just as we have the idiom "a bitter pill to swallow"). Using both terms together was a way of intensifying the expression of emotions.
Zephaniah 1:14 The great day of the LORD is near, near and hastening fast; the sound of the day of the LORD is **bitter**; the mighty man cries aloud there.	Judgment on those who have turned away from God will cause agony and grief.

---

*Destructive choices, traumatic losses,
and the wrongdoing of others all cause grief.
They are all Sources of Bitterness.*

Grieving Bitterness in the Bible

You can experience confusion about "bitterness" when you've forgiven your offender but you still feel the effects of the pain. In our modern Western church cultures, strong feelings are often disparaged, and if you express strong feelings, you might be regarded with condescension or even contempt. This is evidence to some that "you must still be bitter."

But it was different in Bible times. People in Biblical cultures weren't ashamed or afraid to *feel* grief and weren't ashamed or afraid to *express* it.

— The <u>feeling</u> of agony and grief

God made you in such a way that when something traumatizing happens, *you feel it.* If you don't feel it, if you can't feel it or you refuse to feel it, you'll suffer negative results, like becoming divided in soul or becoming physically sick. The people of the Bible felt their grief.

Feelings of Grieving Bitterness in the Bible	Who had the bitter feelings, and why?
Job 10:1 I loathe my life; I will give free utterance to my complaint; I will speak in the **bitterness** of my soul.	Job felt the grief of losing his family members, material goods, and health.
Isaiah 38:15 I walk slowly all my years because of the **bitterness** of my soul.	Hezekiah felt grief in his soul because of his terminal illness.
I Samuel 22:2 And everyone who was in distress, and everyone who was in debt, and everyone who was **bitter** in soul, gathered to [David].	These men felt grief because of their terrible circumstances.
I Samuel 30:6 And David was greatly distressed, for the people spoke of stoning him, because all the people were **bitter** in soul, each for his sons and daughters.	The people felt great grief because their family members had been taken captive by the Amalekites.

— The <u>expression</u> of agony and grief

Many Western churches have adopted a Stoic attitude that our feelings aren't important and should be squelched, emphasizing that feelings should be subjected to reason. But when you feel deeply, it's appropriate for your feelings to come out. This is true even if you've forgiven the person who caused the problem.[47]

For the people of the Bible, their *feelings* of agony and grief came out in an agonizing *expression* of their agony and grief.

Expressions of Grieving Bitterness in the Bible	Why were they expressing their bitterness?
Genesis 27:34 [Esau] cried out with an exceedingly great and **bitter** cry and said to his father, "Bless me, even me also, O my father!"	Esau expressed the heart-wrenching grief he felt at the betrayal by his brother and loss of the blessing.
I Samuel 1:10 She was deeply distressed and prayed to the LORD and wept **bitterly**.	Hannah expressed the agonizing grief she felt at her inability to have a child.
Esther 4:1 When Mordecai learned all that had been done, he tore his clothes and put on sackcloth and ashes, and . . . he cried out with a loud and **bitter** cry.	Mordecai lamented because of the terrifying declaration of the king that all Jews would be destroyed.
Isaiah 22:4 Look away from me; let me weep **bitter** tears; do not labor to comfort me concerning the destruction of the daughter of my people.	Isaiah mourned the destruction of his people so much that anyone trying to comfort him would be wasting time.
Jeremiah 6:26 Put on sackcloth, and roll in ashes; make mourning as for an only son, most **bitter** lamentation, for suddenly the destroyer will come upon us.	Jeremiah told the people to lament because destruction was coming.
Jeremiah 31:15 "A voice is heard in Ramah, lamentation and **bitter** weeping. Rachel is weeping for her children; she refuses to be comforted for her children, because they are no more."	The people would cry out with great lament and refuse to be comforted because of their destruction.
Luke 22:62 And [after denying Jesus, Peter] went out and wept **bitterly**.	Peter mourned and lamented, expressing poignant grief over his denial of his Lord.

---

[47] One of the feelings that can be included in grief, if wrong has been done by another person, is righteous anger. Righteous anger is an emotion that energizes a person to take action against evil for the glory of God (such as David against Goliath) or to help and protect (such as William Wilberforce against Parliament in defense of the slaves).

Understanding grief

— *Grief has been ignored*

Pioneer missionaries to some primitive cultures have found that they have a hard time expressing concepts like redemption, forgiveness, and reconciliation, because there aren't any words for those ideas—those concepts don't even exist in those cultures.

We do still have the word *grief* in our Western culture, but many in the modern Western Christian world have ignored the concept.

For example, what do you do when a well-known speaker writes a book about emotions, and he discusses *bitterness* but leaves out *grief?* That's what has happened in Charles Stanley's book *Emotions: Confront the Lies, Conquer with Truth.* The author writes of a man who suffered the loss of his three-year-old son. The man "became angry toward the Lord, the church, and anyone who crossed his path."[48] Instead of understanding that the man needed someone to help him walk through the grieving process to the other side, Stanley concludes that "bitterness [which he saw as a sinful thing] festered within him."[49]

Bill Gothard is another one who never mentions grief. As part of his teaching on using gratefulness to cure bitterness, he tells a story of a mother whose married daughter called from another country asking for help with her abusive husband. The next day the mother found that her daughter had been murdered by her husband the night before.

How would you advise such a mother with such a grief—losing her daughter at the hands of a wicked man? Bill Gothard told her that she should simply learn to be grateful in order to overcome her bitterness.[50]

---

[48] Charles Stanley, *Emotions: Confront the Lies, Conquer with Truth.* (Howard Books, 2014), p 179.

[49] Ibid.

[50] Bill Gothard, "Basic Seminar, Session 7," www.embassymedia.com. Gothard made it plain that he believed there was no difference between "deep hurt" and bitterness, which he taught to be always sinful and an open door for Satan's work in our lives.

Yet the Bible makes it very clear that though forgiveness is an important part of the Christian life,[51] the bitterness of grief is not sin. Otherwise we would not be told to "weep with those who weep."[52]

— What is grief?

Though the concept of grief is a complicated one, there are an increasing number of Christians who want to try to wrap arms of understanding around it. In his classic book *A Grief Observed,* C. S. Lewis made that effort to describe the wide and almost crazy-making range of strong emotions encompassed in the word *grief*:

> No one ever told me that grief felt so like fear. I am not afraid, but the sensation is like being afraid. The same fluttering in the stomach, the same restlessness, the yawning. I keep on swallowing.
>
> At other times it feels like being mildly drunk, or concussed. There is a sort of invisible blanket between the world and me. I find it hard to take in what anyone says. Or perhaps, hard to want to take it in. It is so uninteresting. Yet I want the others to be about me. I dread the moments when the house is empty. If only they would talk to one another and not to me.
>
> There are moments, most unexpectedly, when something inside me tries to assure me that I don't really mind so much, not so very much, after all. Love is not the whole of a man's life. I was happy before I ever met H. I've plenty of what are called "resources." People get over these things. Come, I shan't do so badly. One is ashamed to listen to this voice, but it seems for a little to be making out a good case. Then comes a sudden jab of red-hot memory, and all this "commonsense" vanishes like an ant in the mouth of a furnace.

---

[51] Forgiveness deserves its own section, but won't be getting it in this book.
[52] Romans 12:15.

On the rebound one passes into tears and pathos. Maudlin tears. I almost prefer the moments of agony. These are at least clean and honest. But the bath of self-pity, the wallow, the loathsome sticky-sweet pleasure of indulging in it—that disgusts me....

And no one ever told me about the laziness of grief. Except at my job—where the machine seems to run on much as usual—I loathe the slightest effort. Not only writing but even reading a letter is too much. Even shaving. What does it matter now whether my cheek is rough or smooth?[53]

Notice that in this poignant depiction of his own grief after his wife's death, Lewis describes a gamut of emotions and strange feelings involved in grief: fear, restlessness, confusion, dullness of senses, loneliness, wildly shifting feelings, sharpness of memories, despair, sadness, anger, self-hatred, depression, and even a kind of dissociation, as he is able to function in his job but not in his leisure time.

Even cases of "simple" grief are complicated, because no grief is truly simple.

— *Case study: Naomi*

Have you ever heard Naomi in the book of Ruth being used as an example of someone who was in sin because of her bitterness?

Did you ever simply feel sorry for her?

Here's the story: Naomi and her husband and two sons left their home of Bethlehem during a time of famine, to live in Moab. By the time she was ready to return to Bethlehem, Naomi had suffered the loss of three family members: her husband and sons were all dead.

Naomi had no hesitations
in expressing her feelings of grieving bitterness.

---

[53] C. S. Lewis, *A Grief Observed* (HarperOne, 2009), pp 15-17.

Speaking to her daughters-in-law, Ruth and Orpah, Naomi said in Ruth 1:13, "It is exceedingly bitter to me for your sake that the hand of the LORD has gone out against me." When she returned home, she said to the people of Bethlehem in Ruth 1:20, "Do not call me Naomi; call me Mara ['bitter'], for the Almighty has dealt very bitterly with me."

For the people who see bitterness as always sinful, Naomi's bitterness must have been sin. Some have compared her with Joseph from the book of Genesis, in whose story no bitterness is recorded. Joseph's brothers had sold him into slavery, but in Genesis 50:20 he said to them, "As for you, you meant evil against me, but God meant it for good."

You may have been told that Naomi should have had Joseph's attitude. (And you may have been told that you should too.)

But let's think about those two stories....

Genesis 50:20 is a beautiful verse reminding all of us that our gracious God is ultimately in control and can bring good even out of evil. But there's one thing to remember about that Bible verse.

When Joseph said it, he was at the end of his story.

When Joseph spoke Genesis 50:20, "You meant it for evil, but God meant it for good," he could look back over the whole story of his life and see how God had held him, even through evil events, right to where he was at that point.

But there was a time, when Joseph was only seventeen, when he experienced the bitterness of betrayal by family members and being sold into slavery, with fetters put on his feet and an iron collar around his neck.[54] There was a time when he experienced the bitterness of an unjust accusation from the woman whose husband he served as a slave. There was a time when he languished for years in a dungeon for a crime he never committed. There was a time when one man who was released promised to speak a good word for Joseph and get him out, *but he forgot about him for two more years.*

---

[54] Psalm 105:18.

Do you think there could have been times during those thirteen years of slavery and imprisonment—when Joseph had to see only with the eyes of faith, believing what God had shown him, with no physical evidence at all—when he may have wept tears of grief for his homeland, for his father and mother and the one brother who loved him?

During that time, those confident words of Genesis 50:20 might not have so quickly risen to his lips. It would have been very natural if, even while he hoped in the goodness of God, he had experienced grief.

When Naomi left Moab and returned to Bethlehem at the beginning of the book of Ruth, she was in the middle of her story. And we all know we shouldn't judge a book by its middle.

Naomi felt as if she had no hope or future.
But her story didn't end there.

In the middle of Naomi's story, Ruth came as an unlikely heroine to walk beside her and help her hold out hope for something better than the bitter experiences Naomi had endured. By the time she came to the end of her life, Naomi was able to see true redemption come to her family, in the most unlikely of ways.

Naomi couldn't have predicted that the son of Ruth and Boaz she held in her arms would one day be the grandfather of David, the greatest king of Israel, and an ancestor of Jesus Himself. She couldn't have predicted that her son-in-law Boaz would one day be seen as a type of Christ. She couldn't possibly have known how far, far greater the plan of God was than the perspective she was able to have.

But I do think that at the end of her life, she, like Joseph, could look back over the whole story, the love story of Ruth and Boaz, and see how God had held her, even through evil events, right to where she was at that point. Like Joseph, she could say, "God meant it for good."

But when someone is in the middle of the story, she might just need to cry. She might need to weep bitter tears.

> *And she might need someone nearby*
> *who can hold out hope in the goodness of God*
> *without scolding her for being bitter.*

— Case study: Job

Bill Gothard upheld Job as a man who gives us an example of refusing bitterness, with a "fantastic, mature outlook,"[55] because after suffering many tragic losses, in Job 1:21 he said, "The Lord gave, and the Lord has taken away; blessed be the name of the Lord."

Yes, that verse at the beginning of the book shows amazing acquiescence. But does that mean Job never experienced Biblical bitterness?

What about Job 7:11? *"Therefore I will not refrain my mouth; I will speak in the anguish of my spirit; I will complain in the bitterness of my soul."*

What about Job 10:1? *"I loathe my life; I will give free utterance to my complaint; I will speak in the bitterness of my soul."*

Job had lost his family members, all his goods, and his own health. As he journeyed through the grief process, he experienced deep grieving bitterness in his soul.

Jerry Sittser would be another one who knows grief. Like Naomi, he lost three family members: in a tragic car accident, his mother, wife and daughter were all suddenly killed.

Sittser wrote his enduring book *A Grace Disguised: How the Soul Grows through Loss,* to explore grief in a Christian context.

In the chapter entitled "the Terror of Randomness," the author reflects on how very random his tragedy appeared—and the tragedy of others, too.

Then he thinks about this sense of randomness in the story of Job—how must Job have felt when one catastrophic blow after another befell his family?

---

[55] Bill Gothard, "Basic Seminar, Session 7."

Job's story became more understandable and meaningful to me when I tried to stand *inside* his experience, which is possible for anyone who has suffered severe loss. . . .

I . . . realized that Job stopped asking questions not because God was a bully, but because Job finally beheld God's unfathomable greatness in his immediate experience. He had spoken about God; then he came to know God. On meeting the real God, he simply had no more questions to ask. He discovered that God is the answer to all his questions, even questions he had not thought to ask.[56]

This journey of Job's in understanding and knowing God through his grief traversed the entire book of Job, 42 chapters. At the end of the story, Job came to understand more about who God really is. But along the way, during the journey, Job experienced grieving bitterness.

— Grieving bitterness is not sin

When I was a young(er) adult, an older woman in our church lost her husband to cancer. After several months, she was still grieving him. I recoiled inwardly and thought, "She's made him into an idol."

I shudder now about that inward response. I had no understanding then that when a beloved marriage partner dies from a long and happy marriage, natural grieving may go on for several years. But how would someone who hasn't lost something or someone dear to them have known this? It is so rarely preached on in our churches.

A missionary writes of the grief that she and her husband carried after learning that their daughter had been sexually assaulted, with all the traumatic aftermath of such a violation. She poignantly describes the deep sense of isolation and desperate need of companionship in the midst of it.

---

[56] Jerry L. Sittser, *A Grace Disguised: How the Soul Grows through Loss* (Zondervan, 2004), pp 102-103.

> Reader, if you know someone who is grieving, just show up! Hold them. Cry with them. *No words required!* I wanted the whole world to stop and grieve with me.[57]

Lament has become a lost art in Western Christianity. If it were to return into the fabric of our culture, all of us could be deepened through it. If you've experienced great sorrow, you could lament without anyone telling you that you need to hurry up and "get over it." If you haven't experienced great sorrow, you could learn to sit with someone else in grief.

> We are taught that grieving is feeling sorry for yourself, and that real strength is to not show any emotions at all. Because we do not know how to be sad, we want to get to the end-stage of grief; we want the benefits and the results of healing, but we do not want to take the time to move through the often long and painful process of grief. For too long we have been taught that shedding tears is a sign of weakness and that you must not wallow in your sorrow....
>
> As a result of this approach to grief, we have a whole generation of people with unresolved issues, hurts, and pains in their past that have been shallowly dealt with at best, and at worst have been ignored and discounted completely. The result has been an increasingly shallow Christianity and a profound lack of understanding of the nature of God and how, as His people, we are to move and live in a fallen world.[58]

— *Grieving bitterness after abuse*

The grief associated with various kinds of abuse is even less understood in our society. Author Steven Tracy ponders the grief of sexual abuse in the story of Tamar, told in II Samuel chapter 13.

---

[57] Dana McCutchen, "A Missionary Family's Grief," Global Counseling Initiative, October 4, 2015. www.globalcounselinginitiative.com/a-missionary-familys-grief.

[58] Ken Cope, in the foreword to *A Sacred Sorrow Experience Guide* by Michael Card (NavPress, 2009), p 9. Michael Card's work on lament is worth exploring at length.

> The unmitigated tragedy of Tamar's story was revealed in her response to being thrown out of Amnon's house. She tore her long robe—the kind worn by virgins—and put ashes on her head, put her hand on her head, and wept bitterly. All of these actions were cultural signs of grief.... Tamar's dramatic actions (weeping, tearing her dress, putting ashes on her head) were most appropriate expressions of grief over a tremendous loss.[59]

How many people in our society would understand that?

The grief of the betrayal and trauma of domestic abuse at the hands of what was thought to be a trustworthy spouse is something else many in our society don't understand. In a pamphlet entitled "Grief and Loss After Abuse," The Women's Resource Service of Australia mentions that most societies have prescribed cultural norms for appropriate grieving, and abuse isn't one of them.

> Leaving an abusive partner is generally not recognized by society as an experience of grief, so many women are left to mourn very privately or not at all.[60]

The post-traumatic effects of abuse will often include not only grief, but shame and self-blame, not only for the failed relationship, but for the sadness, loneliness, and depression that follow.

> Some people may have been unable to express any grief or sadness for a significant period of time while they were living with abuse. Suppressing grief may have been a survival strategy, especially if a woman's visible crying and sorrow had been a trigger for further abuse from a partner.

---

[59] Steven R. Tracy, *Mending the Soul: Understand and Healing Abuse* (Zondervan, 2008), pp 66, 68.

[60] "Grief and Loss after Abuse," Women's Resource Service, www.wrs.org.au/flex/grief_and_loss_after_abuse/71/1. Accessed September 2012.

Some women have also faced a dilemma about allowing their children to see them visibly upset, and have buried their grief for many years while the children were young or dependent.

For these women, the extent and complexity of their grief and loss may feel overwhelming, even frightening.[61]

In 2015, I coordinated a small conference for sexual abuse survivors (with several domestic abuse survivors present as well). The conference included what I called a Service of Lament.[62] The very idea of this was frightening to some, since they had always been silenced and had not been allowed to grieve all that they had lost. But as one author said,

---

Although there will be weeping in this life, the direction in which we weep is what truly matters.[63]

In our experience of shared grief, grieving together, we sought to weep forward, toward hope, toward the One to Whom each of our tears is precious enough to keep in His bottle.[64]

Though our grief didn't express the same strength of emotion that the ancient Hebrews did, our time of grieving was a first experience for several who came. When people who had been abused "felt permission" to grieve together, God began to move within them in a new way, to show Himself to be a God who is great enough and loving enough to welcome their sorrow, their grief, and their questions.

One woman shared months later that the Service of Lament was the beginning for her of . . .

---

[61] Ibid.

[62] Dale Ingraham first gave me the idea for this, with his service that he called "Blameless in His Eyes," described in his book *Tear Down This Wall of Silence: Dealing with Sexual Abuse in Our Churches* (Ambassador International, 2015).

[63] From Kelly Minter, *Ruth: Loss, Love, and Legacy* (Lifeway Press, 2009).

[64] Psalm 56:8.

> . . . the ability to grasp what lamenting means, to see that there is a place to put those feelings that were so stuffed inside myself that I didn't know they existed. They had seeped out of me constantly, through anxiety or bulimia or cutting or alcohol abuse, but I didn't know the feelings were there. The Service of Lament helped me to see how to take the feelings that overwhelmed and oppressed me, and to know what it meant to lay them onto God. And He took many of them, right there in that room. . . . He took them, and now He carries those feelings, so I don't have to.[65]

She is emphasizing an important point here. . . .

— *Our Good Shepherd is with us in our grieving*

Because of the bitter experiences of many people I care about, I've experienced grieving bitterness myself many times. I've gone through times of weeping bitterly and nearly uncontrollably. I've questioned God in my grief, expressing anger and doubt.

But I know He isn't disturbed by my questions and anger, and I always trust that eventually He will bring me—and the people I cry out for—to the other side of the bitterness and reassure both them and me of His care.

You can expect the Good Shepherd to lead you out of the valley of grieving, that bitter sorrow and mourning, the way He did for Naomi and Job, and the way He has done for many others. But while you're in it, He understands and cares. He—the God who wept outside the tomb of His friend Lazarus[66]—mourns with you.

We can live in hope that our Lord will one day redeem all the brokenness of this sin-cursed world,[67] but He expects you to carry no

---

[65] Personal correspondence, from an attendee at the 2015 Shining the Light conference, used by permission.

[66] This story is told in John 11.

[67] As is described in Romans 8:21.

burden of guilt for grieving bitterness. In it, He is with you, and He loves you.

> **Untwisted Truth from Chapter Three**
>
> - The word *bitterness* has three related meanings.
> - One of them is the source, or cause, of bitterness.
> - A second one is the bitterness felt and expressed in agony and grief.
> - Grieving bitterness is not sin. In your grief, the Lord is with you and cares for you.

CHAPTER 4

I'm told I have a "root of bitterness" or I'm in the "gall of bitterness"

In the chart on page 56, you can see the three kinds of bitterness. The first two we talked about in Chapter 3: you don't need to feel guilty about expressing bitter grief you feel as a result of bitter experiences—in fact, it's the way God made you.

There are many Sources of Bitterness, like life circumstances or our own bad decisions.

But one Source of Bitterness—Destructive Bitterness, a source of grief from another person—is important enough to get its own category. Notice, though, that it's really a sub-category:

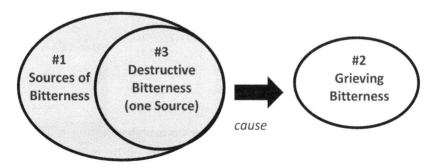

You've probably observed that the people who are accused of sinful bitterness are often the ones who are experiencing Grieving Bitterness.

But that isn't the bitterness that is sinful. The only bitterness that is sinful is #3, Destructive Bitterness.

Surprisingly (at least it was surprising to me), there are very few Scriptures that portray bitterness as clearly negative. So few that we can look at every one of them.

So first, maybe you've been accused of having a "root of bitterness"?

The "root of bitterness" in Hebrews

If you're struggling in an abusive relationship, or still feeling the effects of childhood trauma or betrayal by a friend, someone may accuse you of having that "root of bitterness" by which you will "defile many." This is a way Scriptures are twisted, silencing ones who need to speak.

When I researched sermons and writings about bitterness, I found Hebrews 12:15 referenced again and again . . . and again. This verse is used to tell victims and survivors of abuse, trauma, and betrayal that their primary—and perhaps only—problem is unforgiveness. Here it is:

> *See to it that no one fails to obtain the grace of God;*
> *that no **"root of bitterness"***
> *springs up and causes trouble,*
> *and by it many become defiled;*

Many people, when they read that Scripture, immediately think, "That's talking about unforgiveness, and if I don't get the grace of God to forgive, I'll defile many."

People who already feel contaminated by abuse
become afraid they're in danger of contaminating others.

But here's some untwisting: There's actually no legitimate basis for that interpretation. To untwist this Scripture all the way means we'll have to look at three things: the Old Testament passage it's referring to, the audience it's addressing, and its context.

—The Old Testament reference

When someone asked me what Bible study tools I recommend, I said there were several (lexicons, dictionaries, concordances, etc.), but I told her my favorite Bible study tool is the New Testament, when it referenced the Old. I'm excited to be able to look at an Old Testament Scripture with New Covenant eyes. And then that Old Testament passage will often open up something about the New Testament passage that I hadn't noticed before.

So when I found out this Hebrews passage was referencing a passage from Deuteronomy, you'd better believe I was interested. Here is Deuteronomy 29:18-19.

> *Beware lest there be among you*
> *a man or woman or family or tribe,*
> *whose heart turns away this day from the Lord our God*
> *to go and serve the gods of those nations;*
> *lest there be among you*
> **<u>a root bearing poisonous and bitter fruit,</u>**[1]
> *one who, when he hears the words of this sworn covenant,*
> *blesses himself in his heart, saying,*
> *"I shall be safe, though I walk in the stubbornness*
> *[twisted obstinance] of my heart."*
> *This will lead to the sweeping away of moist and dry alike.*[2]

---

[1] In the KJV it's "gall and wormwood," which suggest not only bad taste, but poison.

[2] This last sentence implies that when this "root" is allowed to stay in the congregation of the Lord, the innocent will suffer as well as the guilty. Jesus may have been hinting at this Scripture when He was on His way to the cross. The Pharisees, those who had assigned Him to death, had certainly thought, "I shall be safe, though I walk in the stubbornness of my heart." But Jesus turned to the people who were bitterly mourning and lamenting, to warn them about the impending destruction of their nation. He said in Luke 23:31 (KJV), "For if they do these things in a green tree, what shall be done in the

In this Deuteronomy passage it's really obvious that the "root" that bears poisonous and bitter fruit isn't a *feeling* deep within the heart. It's a *person*. An actual person, or group of people.³

When Moses wrote this passage in Deuteronomy, he was warning against a kind of poison, a poison that could potentially infect the people of God. The "root of bitterness" has been defined as a way-deep-down-in-your-heart feeling for so long by so many that it may take some time for this untwisting to sink in. It may take some time to understand the implications of this right way of looking at it.

The "root of bitterness" in both Deuteronomy and Hebrews is a *person* in the midst of the congregation, one who produces something poisonously "bitter." This isn't about a secret sin that you need to root out of your own individual heart, hoping that others who are in authority over you can see it when you can't. Moses (and the author of Hebrews) said what needed to be "rooted out" was a *person,* and what he or she needed to be rooted out *from* was the congregation.⁴

The bitterness of this person is described in the Scripture. He or she

- turns away from the Lord God to other gods,
- blesses [exalts] himself in his heart (essentially treating himself like a god), and
- thinks he will be safe, even though he walks in the twisted obstinance of his heart.

---

dry?" I picture Him when He said "green tree," pointing to Himself, and when He said "dry," pointing to those wicked ones who would live to see the complete destruction of their nation, in 70 A.D.

³ "'Root' refers not to a principle in Deuteronomy, but to an individual, to a person given to idolatry. A person also seems to be intended here [in Hebrews]." John Calvin, *Calvin's Commentaries* (Baker Books, 1974), Volume 22, p 400.

⁴ "As in Deuteronomy, so here the bitter root which might spring up and bring forth its poisonous fruit among them was one of their own members who might lead them astray or introduce evil practices and so the whole community . . . might be defiled." W. Robertson Nicholl, editor, *The Expositor's Greek New Testament* (William B. Eerdman's Publishing Company, 1956), Volume 4, p 370.

If this person wasn't rooted out from the congregation, what would happen? How could others be "swept away" (in Deuteronomy) or "defiled" (in Hebrews) by this person?

If other people in the congregation were to begin following someone who exalted himself, they would be in grave danger of being turned aside from the truth.[5] They would be in danger of becoming a gross caricature of what they should have been, swallowing the poison themselves, and then being swept away to call good evil and evil good, putting sweet for bitter and bitter for sweet.[6]

— Who was he speaking to?

Here's another problem. Many modern interpretations of Hebrews 12:15 say this verse is speaking to an individual. "You" (individually) should check for that root of bitterness in "your" (individual) heart.

But that's not the way it is. The entire book of Hebrews was written to a group—the Hebrew Christians. This passage is no different.

The author is saying the *group* of Christians, the *congregation*, should discern the *individual* person within the group who is causing trouble in the way he described, and root him out.[7] If they don't, if they instead follow his poisonous and destructive path, they will experience the agony and grief that comes with departing from the Lord. They will find the hand of the Lord against them for allowing this ungodly person to remain in their midst.

— What about the context?

On the next page is Hebrews 12:15-17.

---

[5] "As one idol-worshipper in a community might bring into it a root of bitter poison [in the Deuteronomy passage], so one apostate from the Christian faith would bring trouble and defilement on the Church." Charles John Ellicott, *Bible Commentary for English Readers* (Cassell and Company, 1930), Volume 8, p 340.

[6] Isaiah 5:20.

[7] The King James translators used *you* for plurals and *thee* or *thou* for singulars, so their readers could easily discern which form was intended.

> *Looking diligently lest any man fail of the grace of God;*
> **lest any root of bitterness springing up trouble you,**
> *and thereby many be defiled;*
> *Lest there be any fornicator, or profane person, as Esau,*
> *who for one morsel of meat sold his birthright.*
> *For ye know how that afterward,*
> *when he would have inherited the blessing, he was rejected:*
> *for he found no place of repentance,*
> *though he sought it carefully with tears.*[8]

In the chart on page 57, Esau is shown to be a Source of Bitterness to his parents, because of his destructive actions in taking heathen women as his wives (one way he showed he didn't value his true birthright). The two problems focused on in this section are fornication and profanity—flip sides of the same problem. (One is elevating the fleshly to a place of exaltation; the other is degrading the holy to a place of defamation.) Esau was displaying the very definition of sin: treasuring what God despises and despising what God treasures.[9] What Esau did, when he treated holy things as if they were meaningless, was *value the temporal* (what he could see) *instead of the eternal.* Because of that, he did not inherit the blessing.

The larger context of the chapter—and the whole book of Hebrews—is to tell believers in Jesus Christ, you're not like that! You've received the spiritual inheritance instead of the physical inheritance.[10] Make sure you don't let a "root of bitterness" (a charming leader who wants to exalt himself) pull you away from it.

Here in the Hebrews reference to Esau you can see echoes of the Deuteronomy passage. Remembering that bitterness is associated with

---

[8] Hebrews 12:15-17 KJV. The topic of repentance deserves its own section, which, alas, it won't be getting in this book.

[9] Holiness, on the other hand, is treasuring what God treasures and despising what God despises.

[10] This is the emphasis in the previous chapter of Hebrews, the great Faith Chapter of the Bible.

poison, we can look at the example of Esau to see that the "root of bitterness" is a person who poisons the congregation by . . .

- turning away from the Lord God to other gods,
- exalting himself in his heart (essentially treating himself like a god),
- thinking he will be safe, even though he walks in the twisted obstinance of his heart,
- valuing the temporal more than the eternal,
- treating holy things (like the spiritual inheritance) as if they're valueless.

So this passage is saying . . .

---

*Those who exalt themselves
and despise the inheritance of Christ
can "trouble" the congregation and poison them
so that many will be defiled.*

The Old Covenant people, the Israelites, were all too often far too much like Esau—valuing what they could see over the greater treasures that they couldn't see. The New Covenant people, the Christians who were being addressed in the book of Hebrews, who were the recipients of that priceless *eternal inheritance*,[11] needed to keep in mind that this could be a danger for them too.

Is it a potential danger for us too? Absolutely, a very real danger.

But the twisting that has taken place with this Scripture to use it as a way to shame and blame those who are struggling with grief has caused another complication: *The real problem isn't being addressed.*

---

[11] Many Scriptures talk about the eternal inheritance—the eternal, abundant life Jesus offers us that begins in the spiritual realm of this life and continues in heaven. In Hebrews alone, besides chapters 11 and 12, the author mentions it in 1:14, 6:17, and 9:15. It is also a common theme in Galatians and Romans, and is mentioned in several other New Testament books.

While writers and speakers are telling you that you need to search your heart for the root of bitterness, which they call unforgiveness, they allow the real roots of bitterness, the self-exalters in positions of authority, to gain more and more ascendancy.

---

*Wolves can come in—
not only the ones that wear sheep's clothing—
but even some who wear shepherd's clothing.*

If you're struggling with grief or trauma from the past, or if you're trying to understand how to submit to authorities that seem to be sucking the life out of you, you might be accused of having a root of bitterness deep within your heart that needs to be identified and rooted out. But that just doesn't match with what this text actually says and means.

Sometimes the people who make these accusations are simply repeating what they've been told, without really meaning to harm you. But sometimes the ones making the accusations are the very ones who *are* in fact the poisonous roots of bitterness within the congregation.

They—and the Twisted Scriptures they present—become a Source of Bitterness to anyone who is affected by them.

***

You also may have been accused of being in the "gall of bitterness." So that's another one we need to look at and untwist.

The "gall of bitterness" in Acts

The whole book of Acts is filled with awesome works of the Holy Spirit. In Acts 8 He had just been accomplishing amazing "acts" in a certain city through Philip, who had been preaching and working miracles. Now the apostle Peter came and laid his hands on the new Christians, for them to receive the Holy Spirit.

Whatever it was that happened when these Christians received the Holy Spirit (this passage doesn't say), one new follower named Simon was so bowled over with astonishment and wonder and awe that he immediately offered to pay Peter to show him how to do the same thing.

But Peter replied to him in Acts 8:20-23,

May your silver perish with you,
because you thought you could obtain the gift of God with money!
You have neither part nor lot in this matter,
for your heart is not right before God.
Repent, therefore, of this wickedness of yours,
and pray to the Lord that, if possible,
the intent of your heart may be forgiven you.
For I see that you are in the gall of bitterness
and in the bond of iniquity.

On a first reading, this seems like a pretty shocking statement. We might have thought Simon had simply made an honest mistake and needed to be taught more completely.

But from Peter's Spirit-inspired words, it's clear that wasn't the case. Peter's words strongly indicate that far from simply misunderstanding, Simon was on his way to hell.[12]

So this was a very serious issue, for sure.

But what was Simon's "bitterness"? Was it unforgiveness, or resentment toward God, as many people preach? Was it discontentment and an unwillingness to accept God's will for his life, as some have preached?[13]

---

[12] Acts 8:13 says that Simon believed Philip and had even been baptized. But here Peter indicated he wasn't a real believer in Jesus Christ. It seems that Simon was like one of those "believers" referred to in John 2:23-25, which says, "many believed in [Jesus'] name when they saw the signs that he was doing. But Jesus on his part did not entrust himself to them, because he knew all people and needed no one to bear witness about man, for he himself knew what was in man." Just like these people, Simon apparently "believed," in a way, but not with faith that put all his trust in Jesus Christ.

[13] Bob Wood's sermon on the gall of bitterness is an example. "Bitterness," April 2010, www.sermonaudio.com.

Again, we can look at the context to help us see plainly what Simon's bitterness was. The full context of Acts 8 tells the story.

Before Philip came on the scene, Simon was a sorcerer who had it made. His supposed "supernatural powers"[14] caused everyone in the city to stand in awe of him and give him highest respect.

But that was before Philip arrived, preaching the good news of Jesus Christ and working miracles. When he did that, the people of the city listened to Philip, believed in Jesus Christ, and were baptized.

That's the backdrop for Peter's harsh words in verses 20-23. Though Simon had made a claim of being a believer in Christ, it seems evident that he simply wanted to restore his former control over the people that he now saw slipping away.

In other words . . .

Simon wanted the gifts of the Holy Spirit without any understanding of the Holy Spirit.

He wanted power without surrender.

He wanted to pay for the ability to work miracles like the ones Peter and Philip exhibited, but wasn't at all interested in the love and transformation essential to it. Instead,

---

Simon wanted to use the Holy Spirit as a commodity to advance his personal position, reputation, and sense of power.

Simon's "bitterness," in fact, doesn't look all that different from Esau's. Or the bitterness the Hebrew Christians were being warned about in Hebrews 12:15. He was valuing the temporal over the eternal, and he wanted to exalt himself.

---

[14] Whether he actually had contact with the evil spirit world or just did "magic tricks" is a subject of debate.

The *gall* (poison) of bitterness in Simon's heart was so deep and so great and so pervasive that Simon did well to tremble at Peter's harsh words. He needed to be delivered from the bond of iniquity and the poison of self-exaltation.

Imagine Peter saying to Simon, "No, no you don't understand. You can't buy it. You can only get it by praying this prayer. Here, repeat after me. . . . Now you can be a leader in the church too." This attitude would have been disastrous. If Simon had been granted powers like Philip's or Peter's without the humility and divine love and life transformation that needed to accompany them, he would surely have become a Source of Bitterness to the people around him, as he exalted himself more and more. Imagine, if their former leader had been able to do miracles similar to those of Philip and Peter, except that these miracles were to exalt himself rather than Christ.

Thinking of this possibility reminded me of some words the prophet Amos spoke to the Israelites:

> *But you have turned justice into poison* [gall]
> *and the fruit of righteousness into wormwood—*
> *you who rejoice in Lo-debar* [literally, an empty and vain "nothing"]
> *who say, "Have we not by our own strength*
> *captured Karnaim for ourselves?"* [15]

When Amos said that, he was speaking to God's people Israel. His context was a pronouncement of judgment on them because of their perversion of justice and righteousness into *poison*. How were these perversions displayed? The people were hungry for riches and power, they exalted themselves and their false gods instead of the true God, they despised and ignored the poor, they disdained God's prophets and other people who spoke the truth to them, and they refused to repent. And all along—this may sound surprising—*they thought God was with them, even while they scorned Him.*

---

[15] Amos 6:12-13.

In context, you can see that the "gall of bitterness" is unrelated to lack of forgiveness or resentment toward God. It has nothing to do with discontentment or an unwillingness to accept God's will. This "poison of bitterness" is about twisting the work of God to exalt oneself and become something it was never meant to be.

Untwisted Truth from Chapter Four

- The "root of bitterness" in Hebrews is not a secret sin in your heart. It is a self-exalting person in the midst of the congregation.
- The "gall of bitterness" in Acts is not the sin of resentment or unforgiveness. It is the sin of wanting to have the "out-working" power of the Holy Spirit without the "in-working" transformation of the Holy Spirit.

CHAPTER 5

I'm afraid I'll be guilty of "Destructive Bitterness"

Can people who have Grieving Bitterness become people with Destructive Bitterness? Yes, certainly. But that problem should be evident by clear indicators in the Word of God. Destructive Bitterness is one Source of Bitterness that causes Grieving Bitterness in others.

Which kind of bitterness?	English definition	Observations	A distinctive name
Bitter feelings, bitter words, bitter actions	full of active hatred, stinging, cutting, harsh, virulent, full of intense overt hostility	In Hebrew and Greek, hatred and anger aren't necessarily implied— only the acting out that <u>causes</u> agony and grief. *This kind of bitterness thus becomes #1 for another person.*	**#3** *Destructive Bitterness* Evildoers "aim bitter words like arrows."

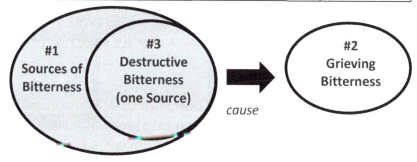

If you've been accustomed to only one meaning for Biblical *bitterness* (resentment resulting from unforgiveness), it may be challenging to think of it with several meanings, even though those meanings are all related. But it might help to look at a word that hasn't been twisted the way *bitterness* has been twisted. In fact, I'll use the word *twisted*.

Three Kinds of "Twisted"

- He/she is so **twisted** (corrupt)
- Now the Scriptures are **twisted** (distorted)
- Now my thinking feels **twisted** (confused)

All those meanings are related, but all of them apply to something slightly different. The twisted (corrupt) person does the twisting of the Scriptures (to distort them) and thus becomes a "Source" of twistedness (confusion) in the oppressed person's mind and spirit.

Besides the "root of bitterness" and the "gall of bitterness," only six other Scriptures refer to Destructive Bitterness. Here they are.

More Scriptures about Destructive Bitterness

— *Psalm 64:2-4*

Hide me from the secret plots of the wicked, from the throng of evildoers, who whet their tongues like swords, **<u>who aim bitter words like arrows</u>**, *shooting from ambush at the blameless, shooting at him suddenly and without fear.*

Now let's think about this one. Enemy nations would have aimed literal, physical arrows, so David wouldn't have been talking about enemy nations here. Since these people aimed *words* like poison arrows, they must have been among David's other enemies, which means, from what we know of David, either King Saul or David's own family members.

What would "bitter words aimed like arrows" sound like? They would probably match with the sins of reviling (or, in the KJV, "railing"), criticizing and insulting with highly abusive language.[1]

These bitter words then became a Source of Bitterness for David, causing him to experience Grieving Bitterness.

Bitter words aimed like poison-tipped arrows
are not expressions of grief,
but are words designed to cause agony and grief
to another person.

If you've aimed bitter words like arrows, then you're guilty of Destructive Bitterness, and it's important for you to repent. But if your words were not intended to cause agony and grief to someone else, then they are not Destructive Bitterness.

— *Habakkuk 1:6*

> For behold, I am raising up the Chaldeans, **that bitter and hasty nation,** who march through the breadth of the earth, to seize dwellings not their own.

The Chaldeans were a bad bunch, so it's safe to acknowledge their "bitterness" as negative. But what kind of negative was it? By what were the Chaldeans characterized?

First of all, they were swift ("hasty") in conquering other nations—that was a big part of how they were able to amass the eventual Babylonian Empire. But was their bitterness a "root attitude of the heart" born of "resisting the grace of God"? That doesn't make sense in this context.

---

[1] Paul warns against this verbal abuser in I Corinthians 5:11 and 6:10, telling that he or she will not inherit the Kingdom of God.

The Chaldeans were "bitter" in the sense that their lust for power, their aggression and violence, spread like poison to become a Source of Bitterness for those they attacked, causing their victims to experience Grieving Bitterness.

— Romans 3:14

*Whose [the wickeds'] mouth **is full of cursing and bitterness.***

This is a quotation of Psalm 10:7, which says, "His mouth is filled with cursing and deceit and oppression." We can see that the "bitterness" of Romans 3:14 matches with the "deceit and oppression" of Psalm 10:7.

In the context of this psalm, the wicked crushes the helpless (vss 2, 8, 9, 10) and believes God will not see or know (vss 3, 4, 11, 13). The poison of his bitterness is overt, not the "very subtle sin" described in modern-day sermons. This description—cursing, deceit, oppression—shows us more clearly the very active Destructive Bitterness of the abuser.

In fact, if you look at more of Psalm 10, you'll find that this person whose mouth is full of bitterness chases after the poor, boasts, and expresses arrogance toward both the Lord and the ones who want to expose him. He says in his heart, "I shall not be moved; throughout all generations I shall not meet adversity" (vs 6).

There's more, but I hope this description rings a bell for you—this is similar to the "root of bitterness" in both Deuteronomy 29 and Hebrews 12, the person who wants to exalt himself and make himself his own god. This person will be a Source of Bitterness, causing Grieving Bitterness for those who have the unfortunate experience of being in his path.

— James 3:13-18

*Who is wise and understanding among you? By his good conduct let him show his works in the meekness of wisdom. **But if you have bitter jealousy and selfish ambition in your hearts**, do not boast and be false to the truth.*

This is not the wisdom that comes down from above, but is earthly, unspiritual, demonic. For where jealousy and selfish ambition exist, there will be disorder and every vile practice.

> *But the wisdom from above is first pure, then peaceable, gentle, open to reason, full of mercy and good fruits, impartial and sincere. A harvest of righteousness is sown in peace by those who make peace.*

This "bitter jealousy" and "selfish ambition" can cause grief to those who are its targets, through the disorder and vile practices they produce.

But the opposite of "bitter jealousy and selfish ambition" described here in James are wisdom, purity, gentleness, reasonableness, mercy, good fruit, impartiality, and sincerity. These qualities describe the righteousness we find in Christ as we trust Him for all our righteousness.

Some of these qualities will be shown by your actions, but some will be shown by your words. This passage reminds us of the importance of speaking the truth with grace.

— *Colossians 3:19*

> *Husbands love your wives, and **do not be bitter** against them.*

The context for the word *bitter* here is that it is the opposite of love. If we were to follow after the other passages of Scripture about bitterness, we could interpret it to say, *"Husbands, love your wives, and do not be a poisonous source of agony and grief to them,"* through your attitudes, words, or actions. This would fit with both the context, the sense of the passage, and the meaning of the word.

— *Ephesians 4:29-32*

> *Let no corrupting talk come out of your mouths, but only such as is good for building up, as fits the occasion, that it may give grace to those who hear. **Let all bitterness** and wrath and anger and clamor and evil speaking **be put away from you**, with all malice. Be kind to one another, tenderhearted, forgiving one another, as God in Christ forgave you.*

This is one of the most preached-on passages about bitterness. It is said that because bitterness is listed first in the list of sins in verse 31, that is evidence to us that it is the "root" of all the other sins that follow. But what do the Scriptures really say?

The context here is about words. We want our words to build up, not tear down. We want to minister grace through our words.

Those words *wrath* and *anger* are both from Greek words for violent passion (the first one implies hard breathing). *Clamor* is yelling. *Evil speaking* is vilifying, slandering, railing, reviling (expressing scorn and contempt through insulting language). *Malice* is wickedness.

So the contrast is between grace-filled words that build people up, and poisonous, evil words that tear people down.

If you think about this context in light of the other Scriptures about bitter words, you can see that this one is reminiscent of Psalm 64—it's easy to imagine the bitter words being aimed like poison-tipped arrows.

Also, if you look at it in the light of Romans 3:14 (and Psalm 10), you can see that Ephesians 4:31 is actually describing *abusive behavior*, not the words that express the pain of having been injured by abusive behavior.[2]

Let's suppose someone who has been oppressed and abused comes to you for help. I know you would listen to her, love her, and try to help in any way you can, but imagine with me for a minute that you don't.

Imagine that instead of building her up and speaking with grace, your heart isn't tender toward her, you accuse her of holding anger, you tell her to get over it, you even become angry and impatient with her.

This kind of communication doesn't minister grace to the hearer. It doesn't edify the hearer. It isn't kind or tenderhearted. In some cases it can even be considered *corrupting talk*.

In a twist of irony,
the one who accuses a person of sinful bitterness
can in reality be
the one who is exhibiting sinful bitterness.

---

[2] Words that express pain from abusive behavior can themselves become abusive, if they are aimed like arrows with the intent to cause grief to another person. This is when the one expressing Grieving Bitterness becomes guilty of Destructive Bitterness.

Looking at Destructive Bitterness in a new light

When you consider these Scriptures that show Destructive Bitterness, as well as the Hebrews 12 and Acts 8 passages from the previous chapter, you'll see that the one who executes Destructive Bitterness will do at least one (usually more) of the following:
- Use his words and/or actions to cause agony and grief to others.
- Despise the inheritance of Christ.
- Practice deceit.
- Practice oppression.
- Experience jealousy and selfish ambition.
- Lust after power, to have the ascendancy and make himself great.
- Want to use the Holy Spirit as a commodity to advance his own personal position, reputation, and sense of power.

Nowhere in the Bible is bitterness shown to be a secret sin, "hidden deep within the heart," which can only be pointed out by those in authority (a teaching that forges it into a tool of religious abuse).

Nowhere in the Bible is sinful bitterness shown to describe the person who has been hurt by an abuser. Instead, Destructive Bitterness paints a picture of the abuser.

Both religious abusers in a church or ministry setting, and those who abuse emotionally, psychologically, and physically within the home can qualify as Biblically "bitter" in the sinful, destructive sense. They then are a Source of Bitterness, causing Grieving Bitterness to others.

When those who need help or need to grieve have to endure accusations of sinful bitterness, this is a bitter pill to swallow. It is a bitter pill that is poisoning all of the church of Jesus Christ.

A response to those who preach their own idea of bitterness

At the beginning of Chapter 3, I showed some common teachings on bitterness. What several of these teachers have done is *eisegesis*, approaching the text with their own preconceived notion of what it should mean, rather than *exegesis,* exploring the text for what it really means.

So now I'd like to go back again to look at what they were teaching.

— *Is bitterness resentment, unforgiveness, and hostility?*

Contrary to what the Scripture Twisters claim (and well-meaning people too), Biblical bitterness doesn't mean you haven't forgiven—you may have forgiven as much as you're capable of at this time, but still feel a confused mixture of the strong feelings of grief from trauma.

Destructive Bitterness is associated with destructive feelings, words and actions, but it is the anger of the abuser who is resisting God and His grace, not the anger of the one who has been abused.

—*Is bitterness hidden deep within an individual's heart?*

Destructive, sinful bitterness is obvious by the words and actions that accompany it. The confused and hurt person who needs help and wants someone to listen, believe, and show compassion[3] doesn't need to be told to repent of something only the spiritual authority can see.

This way of thinking can easily lead to religious abuse.

—*Is bitterness caused by . . .*

Resisting the grace of God? The grace of God comes through Jesus Christ alone. If someone resists Jesus Christ, that person can certainly begin to abuse either himself or others. But the answer doesn't lie in the Christless solutions offered by many preachers,[4] but by trusting in a good God who has paid the price for our sin and shame to redeem us.

Discontent? This could be, if you view Saul's destructively bitter attacks against David as discontent, or the Chaldeans' attacks against other

---

[3] He may also need someone to help untwist his thinking but may not be aware of that at first.

[4] When I say "Christless," I mean in practicality, because many of them will mention Jesus in a tacked-on sort of way. But the way they preach that we should access the grace of God is through works rather than through faith in Jesus Christ.

nations as discontent. The bitterness of the abuser could be construed as discontent, but it goes far deeper than that.

Not dealing with an old hurt, including childhood abuse? Old hurts need to be dealt with. Like an infected wound that needs to be opened and cleansed, if you have an old hurt that continues to haunt you, it needs to be addressed. But instead of Scripture Twisting that tells you to repent of a "root of bitterness," I want to tell you about the love of Jesus Christ, and show it by offering you practical help in the Name of Jesus Christ.

Lack of self-acceptance? This is an example of eisegesis in Acts 8 and has nothing to do with the text or the Biblical concept of bitterness.

A temporal value system? How heartlessly dismissive this is of the true and deep grief felt by people who are going through great loss! Think about someone having lost family members in a tragic accident, or learning that a family member is molesting their daughter, or discovering that the wonderful person they married is really a wolf in sheep's clothing. No, the Grieving Bitterness that many feel and express has nothing to do with temporal values, but with eternal souls—a feeling that God Himself feels, by the way, as He mourns with His children.

And yet this finger-pointing at the "bitter" ones who have been hurt completely ignores the temporal value system of the real "root of bitterness," the person who wants to exalt himself, spreading a poison in the midst of the congregation, valuing his own transient "things that are seen" over the eternal "things that are unseen."[5]

Unmet expectations? Again, let's suppose a woman has married a man that she believes is a good and godly man, but after the wedding she finds him to be self-centered and lacking in empathy, to the degree that he becomes abusive. As time passes she tries to make excuses for him and cover for him, but when she finds that he has physically harmed one of her children, she takes the children and runs to shelter.

---

[5] II Corinthians 4:18.

Was she *expecting* something in her marriage other than what she got? Yes. Was that wrong? No. When she grieves to someone about the pain she feels in an abusive marriage, should she be accused of sinful bitterness? *I hope you say no!*

When Scripture Twisters heap shame on women for expecting to have husbands that will love and care for them, they are themselves practicing Destructive Bitterness.

—Is bitterness the "root cause" of almost every other sin?

This concept is extrapolated from the "root of bitterness" teaching in Hebrews that has nothing to do with hidden sin in the heart.

—What about the solutions given by the Scripture Twisters?

- *They tell you to ask people who are more spiritual than you to point out the bitterness in your heart.*

As they put themselves in the position of being "spiritual enough" to perceive your bitterness, you will remain stuck in your shame and guilt, struggling to hope that God sees and cares.

- *They tell you to confess it, often as an equal or worse sin than the sin committed against you.*

The youth pastor raped your daughter, so now you're angry. But you're told you have no right to be angry; in fact, your anger is worse than the youth pastor's rape.

This accusation is used to shut people's mouths about real wrongs that need to be dealt with, because it is simpler to silence one isolated victim (or family) than it is to address a storm of rumors and truths that can damage the reputation of an important man or an institution.

- *In addition to forgiving, they tell you to refuse to think about any offenses.*

A friend of mine who was in an abusive marriage, in the spirit of some translations of I Corinthians 13:5, kept no record of the wrongs committed against her and tried to forget them. When she went to her pastor for help, he asked what her husband was doing. When she hesitated to say anything, he told her to keep a list the following week and come back. She did, and he rebuked her for keeping a record of wrongs.⁶

It's foolish and even dangerous to tell someone in an abusive situation to refuse to think about offenses. When she's dating the abuser, she needs to be able to recognize red flags. When she's married to him, she needs to learn to understand the pattern of abuse while trying to protect herself and her children.

"Keeping no record of wrongs" is a disputed translation of this passage, one that can lead to erroneous conclusions that have been used to keep abuse victims silent. Paul himself, the one who wrote it, kept a record of the wrongs done to him by Alexander the coppersmith, which he detailed to Timothy in II Timothy 4:14-15. Perhaps a more accurate translation, and consistent with Paul's own actions, would be to say, "Love infers no evil when no evil is obvious."⁷

Keeping a record of wrongs, though it can sometimes be used to hurt someone by reminding them of their minor offenses, can also be a way for a person in an abusive situation to see patterns, to help friends and counselors understand what's happening, to stay sane, and eventually to get to a safe place.

- *They tell you to be like Joseph.*

As I mentioned in the section about Naomi, Joseph was at the end of his story when he said, "As for you, you meant evil against me, but God meant it for good." I pray that if you're going through bitter experiences,

---

⁶ Though the King James translates I Corinthians 13:5 as "thinketh no evil" and the ESV says "is not irritable or resentful," other versions of the Bible, such as the NIV, translate this clause as "keeps no record of wrongs."

⁷ Matthew Henry says of this passage that love "does not reason out evil or charge guilt upon them by inference and innuendo, when nothing of this sort appears open." www.biblestudytools.com/commentaries/matthew-henry-complete/1-corinthians/13. Adam Clarke says of this passage that love "gives every man credit for his profession of religion, uprightness, godly zeal, etc., [when] nothing is seen in his conduct or in his spirit inconsistent with this profession." www.sacred-texts.com/bib/cmt/clarke/co1013. Both of these respected commentators clearly indicate that if by word or action a man shows himself to be a hypocrite, this passage does not apply.

especially at the hands of poisonously destructively bitter people, you'll one day be able to reach a perspective where you can say, "I know God meant it for good." But if right now you are in Grieving Bitterness, there is no sin in that. I pray that you'll have good friends to help you find hope in the Lord and "weep forward."

Responding rightly to bitterness

Sources of Bitterness cause bitter experiences for all of us—it's part of the human condition. In these times, it's appropriate for you to feel Grieving Bitterness and express it with bitter tears and agony.

If the Source of Bitterness, though, is actually another person who is lashing out with destructively bitter words and actions, causing agony and grief as does poison, it's important to recognize where the sinful bitterness lies. I pray that the Church of Jesus Christ will identify this sinful bitterness in their midst and root it out.

As you weep bitter tears, I pray you'll have a good friend to mourn with you. You can also remember as you look to the gentle Shepherd, Rescuer, and Healer, Jesus Christ, that He will heal wounds and wipe away tears and give new beauty where there lay only ashes. The days of this bitterness will pass.

Untwisted Truth from Chapter Five

- One important Source of Bitterness is the person who engages in Destructive Bitterness.
- This person
    - uses his or her words and/or actions to cause agony and grief to others.
    - despises the inheritance of Christ.
    - practices deceit and oppression.
    - lusts after power.

CHAPTER 6

I shouldn't "take up offenses" for others

You may have heard that if you "take up offenses" for others, God won't give you grace for that, and you'll become among the most "bitter" of people (meaning you'll develop a deep "root of bitterness" that will come out in venom directed toward others, so that many of them will be defiled, which thankfully we've already dealt with).

This teaching comes from among the most twisted of Scriptures.

Though many of his followers continue this false teaching, the origin of it belongs squarely at the feet of Bill Gothard.

Bill Gothard's teaching on "taking up offenses"

In Bill Gothard's Basic Seminar Session 7, "Dealing with Hurts / Keys to Forgiveness,"[1] he teaches how wrong it is to "take up offenses" for other people, meaning to feel angry for them about something that has happened to them and to try to help them make it right.

At the first seminar I attended in 1977, in a huge coliseum packed with tens of thousands of people, this teaching was already fully developed, and I took careful and copious notes. Among my notes I see,

---

[1] Available for viewing at www.embassymedia.com.

Taking up Offenses (Psalm 15:3) — the <u>major</u> reason for bitterness (We should never do this)

Maybe I could be excused for being only 19 when I attended . . . and 21 . . . and 22 . . . and 23 . . . and 26. (Did I mention I was a Gothardite?)

– That mysterious Psalm 15:3 reference

There it is, in my 1977 notes, hastily jotted in parentheses without a thought of looking it up (and no time to, since I was dashing off notes as fast as I could) to find out what it actually said, what it actually meant.

> *Psalm 15*
> *O Lord, who shall sojourn in your tent?*
> *Who shall dwell on your holy hill?*
> *He who walks blamelessly and does what is right*
> *and speaks truth in his heart;*
> *who does not slander with his tongue*
> *and does no evil to his neighbor,*
> **<u>nor takes up a reproach against his friend</u>;**
> *. . . He who does these things shall never be moved.*

On the basis of this half of a verse, Bill Gothard has built a major doctrine.

And why would he use the phrase "taking up offenses," when no translation of the Bible translates Psalm 15:3 this way? In place of that Hebrew word in Psalm 15:3, Bible translators have used the word *slur, insult, discredit, speak evil,* or *reproach,* but none of them use the word *offense.* Maybe he substituted this word because it implies something about the speaker's heart—it implies that there is woundedness there, which Bill Gothard (and his followers) would label "bitterness."

But what is the Scripture here actually talking about? A "reproach" is a purposeful effort to discredit someone's good reputation. "Not taking up a reproach" would be more or less the same as "not slandering," "not doing evil," and "speaking truth." So this verse says a godly person won't purposefully seek to harm a (legitimate) good reputation.

Would this mean a man who has a good reputation but is secretly doing evil (i.e., a wolf in sheep's clothing) should never be exposed? Surely that *can't* be what it means, according to all the rest of the Word of God. To expose evil, or to call a brother to repentance, both are consistently in harmony with all the Word of God.

But according to Bill Gothard's teachings (and that of his followers), we run head-on into a doctrine designed to *shut people up.*

– The Basic Seminar teaching

Psalm 15 speaks of "taking up a reproach," as in hurling insults or purposely trying to discredit a good person's reputation. If that were all Gothard were talking about, his teaching would be Biblical.

But it isn't.

His teachings about "taking up offenses" come in the context of his teachings about bitterness and disloyalty.[2] This is a synopsis of what he teaches:

> "Taking up offenses" is one of the most damaging of all causes of "persistent bitterness."
>
> If someone offends me, God will give me the grace to respond to it. But if someone else, "on the sidelines," takes up an offense and becomes bitter against the one who offended me, that person will stay bitter long after I've responded to God's grace. This is because "God doesn't give any grace to the sideliners."
>
> "The most bitter people in the world" are "the ones who are taking up causes, and they don't have any grace to deal with it." . . . "And I just plead with you not in any way to take up offenses for others."

---

[2] Bill Gothard, "Basic Seminar Session 7: Dealing with Hurts / Keys to Forgiveness," Embassy Media video, www.embassymedia.com. Though this teaching is from 1984, it is still as of this writing the current teaching on the Embassy Media website, the distribution point for all of Gothard's seminar teachings.

> There are four "Steps to Disloyalty."[3]
> - An independent spirit.
> - A wounded spirit.
> - Alertness to discontent in other people.
> - A judgmental spirit, "going to the one in charge with a spirit of condemnation, magnifying reports of discontent, violating the Galatians 6:1 teaching to restore such a person in a spirit of meekness, tempted to pride and bitterness."
>
> God wants us to realize that only as we avoid taking up offenses of others will we escape the devastation that comes along with a sequence like that of Absalom, who "took up offenses" for the Israelites[4] and rebelled against his father, leading to his death.

Amazing, isn't it, that he could get all that out of that brief half verse? But wait, there's more. One of Gothard's example stories in this section goes like this:

> Talking with a high schooler, he said, "I am so bitter at my father."
> I said to him, "What did your father do against you?"
> He said, "He didn't do anything to me."
> I said, "Why are you bitter against your father?"
> He said, "Because of what my father did to my mother."
> I said, "Oh, so you're taking up an offense against your father for your mother, is that right?"
> He said, "That's right."

---

[3] I cringe when I hear the words "loyalty" and "disloyalty," because I hear them as potential for spiritual abuse. Authority figures can use the concept of loyalty to the authority as equated with faithfulness to the cause of Christ. More about that at www.bjugrace.com/2014/12/05/are-you-loyal.

[4] Absalom's motivation was not to set things right for the Israelites; it was to gain power for himself so that he could become the king. Absalom is a perfect example of the Destructive Bitterness discussed in Chapters 4 and 5.

The account ends there because Gothard is using it as a springboard for his teaching above. But this scenario deserves to be hovered over.

First of all, I find it hard to imagine that a teenager would say, "I am so bitter at my father." He would probably say "angry" or "mad."

Second, since we're not told what the father did, it's left to our imaginations. It's not hard to imagine, though, since we know what abusive men have done to women. Even Gothard himself, in this very same lecture, tells about a husband who murdered his wife. Let's suppose this was *that* son. Would you really tell him, based on Psalm 15:3, that he is not allowed to be angry about his father's murder of his mother? That he would be sinfully "taking up an offense" if he were to try to do something about it, such as report it to the police and testify in court?

And what if his mother is still alive and his father is abusing her? Are we supposed to tell this son, based on that snippet of a misquoted verse, that he isn't allowed to try to protect his mother from his abusive father? That she has to handle it on her own and he has to stay out of it?

This teaching is unscriptural and appalling.

Gothard directs this false teaching at anyone who tries to point out a wrong in an authority to call him to repentance, or tries to expose a wolf in sheep's (or shepherd's) clothing.

It can even apply to your relationship with non-authorities, as his teachings show elsewhere:

> Mercy-givers *tend to take up an offense for someone who is being hurt by another person,* especially if the one being hurt is a friend. This response can easily lead to bitterness.[5]

What are you supposed to learn from that? That if a friend is being hurt by another person, you're supposed to refuse to listen to your

---

[5] "What are the common characteristics of mercy-givers?" Institute in Basic Life Principles. iblp.org/questions/what-are-common-characteristics-mercy-givers. Boldface in original.

friend, lest you become filled with "bitterness" (which of course he teaches as a root sin from which all kinds of other sins emanate).

– The background of that teaching

As I listened to Session 7 of the Basic Seminar again for this chapter, I was puzzled by something Bill said in passing: "[Taking up offenses] is happening all over, in employment situations especially."[6]

Hmmm, I thought, why did he say that? I would have thought if anything, he would have said especially in churches.

I found my answer at the Recovering Grace website, on their page about not taking up offenses. Apparently while I was attending my first Institute in Basic Youth Conflicts[7] Seminar in 1977, accusations of immorality, sexual abuse, and sexual harassment were swirling inside the benign-looking headquarters in Oak Brook, Illinois. This is what Recovering Grace has said:

> Unfortunately, instead of reducing the hurt and complexity, Gothard actively worked to take advantage of the confusion. He . . . regularly required staff to sign loyalty oaths and to turn over their meeting notes to him as a method of controlling information. Now, over a period of numerous years, he carefully taught new concepts to his staff and employees—with the goal of blocking truthful reports—and extended his teachings nationwide through seminars and alumni booklets.[8]

The teaching about not taking up offenses seems to have been specifically designed to protect ones in authority in his own headquarters who were being accused—including himself. This teaching then found its way to tens of thousands of eager listeners (including yours truly!), many of whom continue to use it to try to silence others even today.

---

[6] Bill Gothard, "Basic Seminar Session 7."

[7] Later renamed the Institute in Basic Life Principles.

[8] "Silencing the Lambs: Taking Up Offenses," *Recovering Grace: a Gothard generation shines light on the teachings of IBLP and ATI.* February 2014. www.recoveringgrace.org/2014/02/silencing-the-lambs-taking-up-offenses.

Imagine being one of Gothard's employees who tried to speak up for one of the young women who were being sexually harassed or worse. Imagine then finding your situation used as an illustration in a lecture about "not taking up offenses," presented to packed coliseums.

> "The most bitter people in the world" are "the ones who are taking up causes, and they don't have any grace to deal with it."[9]

"Taking up offenses" in modern-day teachings

Whenever you hear a sermon or read material about bitterness that mentions "taking up offenses" as one of the causes of bitterness, you can recognize the influence of Gothard.

> Now what is the cause of bitterness? It could be numbers of things . . . Perhaps you take up another person's offense—they have a problem, and you take up their offense.[10]

> One of the more difficult situations is when we intentionally *take up an offense* against another. It is often an offense on behalf of someone we love. God may give grace to the person offended to overcome the offense, but because the offense was not ours, we may *not have the grace* to forgive and walk out of the situation ourselves.[11]

> [R]efuse to take up offenses for the hurts of others. . . . But also you need to be very careful not to take up offenses for the hurts of others. . . . Be very careful to refuse to take up an offense for someone else's hurt. That's their issue, that's their deal with God, you stay out of it. Don't let it affect your heart.[12]

---

[9] Gothard, "Basic Seminar Session 7."

[10] Steve Pettit, "Put Away Bitterness," January 2015, www.sermon-audio.com.

[11] Bob Mumford, *Mysterious Seed: Maturing in Father's Love* (Destiny Image Publishers, 2011), p 309. Italics in original.

[12] Paul Tautges, "Bitter Root, Rotten Fruit," November 2011, www.sermon-audio.com. Yes, all three similar statements were in the same spoken paragraph.

> It's important to remember . . . boundaries when discussing sin in a group setting. . . . Confess your own sin—not someone else's. . . . If someone else sinned against you in a particular situation, you don't need to supply those details and cause someone else in the group to stumble by taking up an offense.[13]

This is another one of those Twisted Teachings without Scriptural support. In fact, the Scriptures teach exactly the opposite.

And the historical precedent is quite impressive.

And the need is great for those who will advocate for others in the Church of Jesus Christ.

"Taking up causes" in the Bible

Because Bill Gothard equates the terms "taking up offenses" and "taking up causes," using them interchangeably, I'll do the same.

– Direct admonitions in Scripture

With one snippet of a Bible verse taken out of context and misinterpreted ("nor takes up a reproach against his friend"), Bill Gothard has swept away with a flick of his finger all the many Scriptural passages that call God's people to take up the cause of the offended.

Proverbs 31:9
Open your mouth, judge righteously,
defend the rights of the poor and needy.

Proverbs 29:7
A righteous man knows the rights of the poor;
a wicked man does not understand such knowledge.

---

[13] Nancy Leigh DeMoss, *Holiness: The Heart God Purifies* (Moody Publishers, 2005), p 185. One woman found that she couldn't tell her small group about the abuse-related flashbacks and nightmares she was struggling with, because they didn't want to hear about the sin of someone else.

Psalm 82:2-4
How long will you judge unjustly and show partiality to the wicked? Selah
Give justice to the weak and the fatherless;
maintain the right of the afflicted and the destitute.
Rescue the weak and the needy;
deliver them from the hand of the wicked.

Leviticus 19:15
You shall do no injustice in court.
You shall not be partial to the poor or defer to the great,
but in righteousness shall you judge your neighbor.

Isaiah 58:6-7
Is not this the fast that I choose:
to loose the bonds of wickedness, to undo the straps of the yoke,
to let the oppressed go free,
and to break every yoke?

Isaiah 1:17
Learn to do good;
seek justice, correct oppression;
bring justice to the fatherless, plead the widow's cause.

Jeremiah 5:26-28
For wicked men are found among my people;
they lurk like fowlers lying in wait.
They set a trap; they catch men.
Like a cage full of birds, their houses are full of deceit;
therefore they have become great and rich;
they have grown fat and sleek.
They know no bounds in deeds of evil;
they judge not with justice the cause of the fatherless, to make it prosper,
and they do not defend the rights of the needy.

Jeremiah 22:3
Thus says the Lord: Do justice and righteousness,
and deliver from the hand of the oppressor
him who has been robbed.

Repeatedly and consistently, the Bible calls us to stand with the weak and oppressed, to speak out for those who for one reason or another can't speak for themselves. God is a God of justice and mercy, and He calls us to walk in justice and mercy with Him, to have His heart, His compassion and empathy.

Let's say, for example, a friend entrusts to you a description of her childhood sexual abuse at the hands of her father, the man she should have been able to trust above all other men. If you then go before the Lord and weep and cry out, you're simply feeling the Christ-like empathy that's part of what it means to be made in the image of God. If you feel "bitterness," it's the Grieving Bitterness discussed in Chapter 3.

Or let's say you help a friend escape from an abusive and dangerous husband, or you call the police on a man who has molested a child. By Gothard's definition this would be "taking up an offense." But instead, you're actually "working out" the righteousness God has called you to in Philippians 2:12.

– Examples in Scripture

Besides all those direct exhortations, the Scriptures also contain a number of examples of people who took up causes of those who had been silenced through oppression.

The prophet Ezekiel, when God told him to cry out against the wicked who dared to oppress the weak, didn't say, "But Lord, that would be taking up offenses, and I don't want to become one of the most bitter people in the world!" Ezekiel 22:29 is only one example of his bold restatement of the words the Lord gave him:

The people of the land have practiced extortion and committed robbery.
They have oppressed the poor and needy,
and have extorted from the sojourner without justice.

The prophet Nathan, when God told him to go expose David's sin of abusing Bathsheba for his own sinful pleasure and having her husband killed, didn't say, "But Lord, You said I'm not supposed to take up offenses for those who have been hurt!" Instead he said directly to David, in II Samuel 12:7, "You are the [guilty] man."

The book of Esther tells how Queen Esther, on hearing that her people were destined to be slaughtered, didn't say, "Well, I'm the queen and I'll be fine, so this isn't my battle to fight. If I take up the cause of my people I won't have any grace to deal with it, and I'll just get bitter." No, she saw the injustice occurring and moved forward to wisely remedy it.

The apostle James, when he saw the rich men who withheld their laborers' wages by fraud, didn't say, "Well, it's not *my* wages they're withholding, so I can't get involved." Instead, he said, in James 5:1-6,

> *Come now, you rich,*
> *weep and howl for the miseries that are coming upon you.*
> *Your riches have rotted and your garments are moth-eaten.*
> *Your gold and silver have corroded,*
> *and their corrosion will be evidence against you*
> *and will eat your flesh like fire.*
> *You have laid up treasure in the last days.*
> **Behold, the wages of the laborers who mowed your fields,**
> **which you kept back by fraud,**
> **are crying out against you,**
> **and the cries of the harvesters have reached the ears of the Lord of hosts.**
> *You have lived on the earth in luxury and in self-indulgence.*
> *You have fattened your hearts in a day of slaughter.*

And my favorite, our Lord Jesus. He saw the Pharisees devouring the houses of the widows, the very segment of society most vulnerable and most in need of protection, in a kind of first-century real-estate shell game. Our Lord didn't say, "Well, they're not devouring *my* house, since I don't have one, so this isn't my battle to fight. I'll set the right example about not taking up the causes of others."

Far from it.

> *"But woe unto you, scribes and Pharisees, hypocrites!*
> *for ye shut up the kingdom of heaven against men:*
> *for ye neither go in yourselves,*
> *neither suffer ye them that are entering to go in.*
> ***Woe unto you, scribes and Pharisees, hypocrites!***
> ***for ye devour widows' houses,***
> ***and for a pretence make long prayer:***
> ***therefore ye shall receive the greater damnation.***
> *Woe unto you, scribes and Pharisees, hypocrites!*
> *for ye compass sea and land to make one proselyte,*
> *and when he is made,*
> *ye make him twofold more the child of hell than yourselves."*
> *Matthew 23:13-15 KJV*

Besides the widows, Jesus took up the cause of all the people being blinded by the Pharisees' false teachings. He did not leave them to try to figure out the truth on their own and then try to help themselves.

In his Basic Seminar teaching, Bill Gothard distinguishes the one who has been offended from the "sideliners." Those, he says, are the people who shouldn't get involved in trying to set things right because they won't receive grace from God and thus will become bitter, so they should "not in any way take up offenses for others."[14]

And yet the sideliner is what none of us is called to be.
We are called to come alongside each one who is hurt or grieving.

The story of the Good Samaritan in Luke 10 gives an example. The priest and Levite saw the man who had been wounded by robbers, but walked on by. Only the Samaritan helped. According to Bill Gothard's definition, they were all "sideliners." But one of them got involved.

---

[14] Bill Gothard, "Basic Seminar Session 7: Dealing with Hurts / Keys to Forgiveness," Embassy Media video, www.embassymedia.com.

If the traveler had been traveling with a child that was kidnapped by these robbers, and if the Samaritan had gone into the hills to rescue that child from the robbers, he would have been "taking up a cause" in the very way Gothard and his followers decry. But he would have been fully right to do so. The "sideliners" become involved in the Name of Jesus Christ.

"Taking up causes" in history

> "The most bitter people in the world" are "the ones who are taking up causes, and they don't have any grace to deal with it."[15]

Suppose Bill Gothard or one of his followers had been standing with William Wilberforce while he was learning details about the horrors of the slave trade through which many of his fellow Parliamentarians (some of them Christians) were prospering. Would Bill have warned him that he was only a "sideliner" who wouldn't be able to receive grace from God to fight someone else's battle? As Wilberforce took up the cause of fighting the slave trade for the next thirty years until it was eradicated, would Gothard have told him he was simply "bitter"?

Would Bill Gothard or one of his followers have told Amy Carmichael that she would become one of "the most bitter people in the world" if she followed through with writing the book *Things As They Are* to alert the people of England to the rampant child prostitution in India?[16]

And what about E.C. Bridgman, the first missionary to China, who let his fellow Englishmen know how English merchants were bringing the Chinese into addiction to opium, one of the "greatest evils afflicting Chinese society"?[17] Only a bitter sideliner?

And yet another story of lesser-known offense-takers:

---

[15] Bill Gothard, "Basic Seminar Session 7."

[16] Amy Carmichael, *Things As They Are: Mission Work in Southern India* (Morgan & Scott), 1903.

[17] Michael C. Lazich, "American Missionaries and the Opium Trade in Nineteenth-Century China," *Journal of World History*, Vol. 17, No. 2 (June 2006), pp 197-223.

Colonists in both French and Belgian Congo had forced villagers to extract rubber from the jungle. As punishment for not complying, they burned down villages, castrated men, and cut off children's limbs. In French Congo, the atrocities passed without comment or protest, aside from one report in a Marxist newspaper in France. But in Belgian Congo, the abuses aroused the largest international protest movement since the abolition of slavery.

Why the difference? . . . Among those missionaries were two British Baptists named John and Alice Harris who took photographs of the atrocities—including a now-famous picture of a father gazing at his daughter's remains—and then smuggled the photographs out of the country. With evidence in hand, they traveled through the United States and Britain to stir up public pressure and, along with other missionaries, helped raise an outcry against the abuses.[18]

These stories could be multiplied many times over. These Christians were doing only what God had called them—and us—to do, in seeing wrongs and seeking to be involved in making them right.

"Few [missionaries] were in any systemic [sic] way social reformers," says Joel Carpenter, director of the Nagel Institute for the Study of World Christianity at Calvin College. "I think they were first and foremost *people who loved other people.* They [cared] about other people, saw that they'd been wronged, and [wanted] to make it right."[19]

Bill Gothard's idea that those who "take up causes" will not receive grace to deal with it . . . well, it's just not in the Bible anywhere. It's a

---

[18] Andrea Palpant Dilley, "The Surprising Discovery about Those Colonialist, Proselytizing Missionaries," *Christianity Today,* January 8, 2014. www.christianitytoday.com/ct/2014/january-february/world-missionaries-made.

[19] Ibid. Italics added.

teaching of his own invention that has been picked up by others who have been influenced by him.

Instead, these Christians who took up causes for others lived their lives like Jesus, with compassion and empathy. They loved. They fought tirelessly and sometimes to the detriment of their own health to bring justice and equity to the lives of the people they were called to and cared about.

I get the impression that God gave them grace to deal with it.

"Taking up causes" in Christian families, churches, and ministries

– Crying out for justice

Jeff Crippen and Dale Ingraham are pastors who have taken up the causes of others. Jeff, through his A Cry for Justice ministry[20] and books *A Cry for Justice*[21] and *Unholy Charade*,[22] and Dale through his Speaking Truth in Love ministry and his book *Tear Down this Wall of Silence*.[23] I've been privileged to partner with both of them in their work, as they cry out for the church at large to pay attention to the wolves and the bleeding sheep in their midst.

– Advocating in the Southern Baptist Convention

In *Tear Down this Wall of Silence,* Dale Ingraham mentions Christa Brown's book *This Little Light*[24] about sexual abuse and cover-ups in the Southern Baptist Convention. Christa advocated tirelessly for many

---

[20] www.cryingoutforjustice.com.

[21] Jeff Crippen and Anna Wood, *A Cry for Justice: How the Evil of Domestic Abuse Hides in Your Church* (Calvary Press, 2012).

[22] Jeff Crippen with Rebecca Davis, *Unholy Charade: Unmasking the Domestic Abuser in the Church* (Justice Keepers Publishing, 2015).

[23] Dale Ingraham with Rebecca Davis, *Tear Down This Wall of Silence: Dealing with Sexual Abuse in Our Churches (an introduction for those who will hear)* (Ambassador International, 2015).

[24] Christa Brown, *This Little Light: Beyond a Baptist Preacher Predator and His Gang* (Foremost Press, 2009).

years asking the SBC to establish a database of sexual offenders who were in ministry at the time of their assault and who had admitted to their offense but had never been prosecuted. At every turn in her efforts, Christa was stonewalled, but her failure to see this database established was certainly not for lack of trying.

The assault on Christa herself had occurred decades earlier. The efforts detailed in her book to bring the SBC to do all they could to shine the light of truth on abuse—those efforts were not for herself. She wanted to protect others.

She was "taking up a cause."

– Advocating one soul at a time

Many victims and survivors of sexual abuse never spoke about their abuse until they found that someone else, often a younger sibling, was also being abused. At that point, they bravely "took up a cause" and sought help in exposing the abuser and protecting the other person.

One woman, escaping from an abusive husband with her six children, expressed great thanks to a friend (who had also been in an abusive marriage) who "took up the cause" of trying to help the woman's church understand her abusive situation. In a time when the woman herself was so traumatized she found it difficult to think, this friend spent hundreds of hours listening, understanding, and advocating. Her adult children also obtained copies of Jeff Crippen's books *A Cry for Justice* and *Unholy Charade,* so they could also be educated in domestic abuse and advocate for others in churches as well.

– If Christians fail to advocate?

Christians who believe they should never "take up a cause" won't see any reason to become educated about abuse. They will refuse to think about the wolves in sheep's (and shepherd's) clothing that hide in our churches. They will remain in willful blindness.

If you've spoken out about abuse, you may have been told to be quiet (not "taking up an offense") and let the survivors speak for themselves.

But in that case, those abuse survivors may very well think, where is everyone else? Why are we the only ones speaking to the Christian community? Where are all the other Christians?

If people who have been oppressed don't see Christians caring, helping, loving, and advocating for them, they won't see the hands and feet of Jesus at work for them.

But if they do see us caring and speaking out to help right those wrongs, we will see a great difference.

*If Christians advocate,
if Christians take up causes of those who are being abused,
then we will be like Christ, who is the true Rescuer.*

Final thoughts

Back when I posted on my own devotional blog about how right it can be to take up offenses for others,[25] I received the following comment:

> I too, attended the [Gothard] seminars and I never got the impression that "not taking up offenses" meant to blindly and idly stand by while millions are starving or are used, abused, exploited, and rejected. I understood it to mean simply that I should not become angry at someone for what they have done or said to someone I know. It is not my place to be angry for or on behalf of someone else, someone who has a voice and can take care of the issue on their own, if they choose to. We ARE to be a voice for those who have no voice, to help those in dire need.

Though my post hadn't mentioned being angry, I'm not opposed to righteous anger (anger that energizes to speak for and help the oppressed), so this was my reply:

---

[25] Rebecca Davis, "Taking up offenses." Here's the Joy, February 2014. www.heresthejoy.com/2014/02/taking-up-offenses.

Thank you for your thoughts. From what you've written, it sounds like you're saying I can take up a cause on behalf of people I don't know, but shouldn't take up a cause on behalf of people I know. Or maybe that I can be righteously angry in a general way when I'm thinking about millions of people, but not in a specific way when I'm thinking about one individual.

Bill Gothard allegedly used the unbiblical teaching of not taking up offenses to exploit people under him and to fire people who were disloyal to him. Others who may have thought those individuals were being mistreated dared not speak up lest they be guilty of taking up offenses. This kind of intimidation is actually common practice in cult-like environments.

If someone is traumatized by abuse, then it may be a long time before she understands how to use her voice. She may be so spiritually abused that she may think it a sin to actually do something about the evil that has happened to her. She may need someone to take up her cause for her as an advocate. This I wouldn't hesitate to do, even if it's someone I know.

This is what Jesus did, and we're called to be like Him: to call Christians to repentance and to cry out against the evildoers of our day.

If you "take up a cause" for someone, you can ask God for enough grace to deal with what you're called to do, and you can most certainly expect it, just like William Wilberforce, Amy Carmichael, and so many others.

If you've been through great trials, it's a natural and God-given desire to want to use what you've learned to help others. When you know for sure it's a good thing, a Christ-like thing, to take up causes for others, you can do so with dignity, always asking God for the outpouring of the grace of Christ and the power of the Holy Spirit in doing it. We walk in the path to which Christ has called us, asking Him to show us the work He wants us to do. We do it in humble submission to the King of Kings and Lord of Lords, the Sovereign to whom all of us—including every abusive person—will one day answer.

We do it because we walk in the footsteps of our Savior, Jesus Christ, the Good Shepherd who came to rescue lambs from wolves.

Untwisted Truth from Chapter Six

- "Taking up causes" in advocating for those who need help is a Scriptural thing to do. This is one way Christians can show the love of Christ to others.

BUT NOT NECESSARILY THE END

Final words

God gave us the Scriptures as a source of hope and encouragement for us, to show us the great salvation we have through Jesus Christ. But some Christian leaders have twisted some of them, resulting in bondage for many of God's people.

Well-meaning teachers have also presented these twisted ideas, without realizing how wrong the teachings are or the harm they're doing. By default, they view their teachings as accurate. They haven't taken the time to understand the implications of their teachings and give the Scriptures a fresh look.

When you read a book to untwist Scriptures that have been twisted in your mind for a long time, you may find that they might not all untwist on the first reading. The untwisting may happen bit by bit or even in an epiphany, sometimes months after you've read it.

One thing I always seek to remember in reading and interpreting the Scriptures is that Almighty God is perfectly represented in Jesus Christ. Hebrews 1:3 tells us He is "the radiance of the glory of God and the exact imprint of his nature." That "exact imprint of his nature" can be roughly translated "the engraving on his under-establishment."

I think of it as Jesus being *the features on the face of God.*

Jesus loved the weak and oppressed. He hated hypocrisy and arrogance and abuse. He died for all who would trust in Him. He rose again and is seated at the right hand of God so that anyone who trusts in Him can walk in the same power in which He walked.

He is the Living Word that the written Word is there to point to and magnify.

And *that's* Untwisted Truth.

*"You search the Scriptures
because you think that in them you have eternal life;
and it is they that bear witness about me."*
John 5:39

About the author

Rebecca Davis, a writer and editor with a passion to help the oppressed, collaborated with Jeff Crippen on *Unholy Charade: Unmasking the Domestic Abuser in the Church* and with Dale Ingraham on *Tear Down This Wall of Silence: Dealing with Sexual Abuse in Our Churches (an introduction for those who will hear)*.

Since 2006 Rebecca has been studying and learning about different kinds of abuse, especially through the first-person experiences of many of her amazing friends. For about thirty years longer than that, she has been an avid student of the Scriptures. She has enjoyed teaching truth to many through the years, to groups as large as five hundred and as small as four or five, about topics as diverse as the realities of abuse, hope through the grief of Alzheimer's, miracles and gospel opportunities in the lives of missionaries, and the true freedom and gracious life transformation to be found in Christ.

Rebecca enjoys getting together for coffee with friends, listening to their stories, and offering hope through Jesus Christ. She has been married to her wise and good husband Tim for over thirty years, and together they have four children and two grandchildren. You can connect with her at www.heresthejoy.com.

Made in United States
North Haven, CT
30 April 2022